California Southern District

COURT AND CHAMBERS PRACTICE MANUAL

DISTRICT COURT
Selected General Orders

INDIVIDUAL JUDGES
Procedures and Practices
Chambers Rules and Standing Orders
Scheduling Information
Chambers and Biographical Information

Mid-2012 Edition

Compiled by Practicing Attorneys
Meliora Law

This publication is created to provide accurate and authoritative information concerning
the subject matter covered. It is sold with the understanding that the publisher is not
engaged in rendering legal or other professional advice. If legal or other expert
advice is required, the services of a competent professional should be sought.

Printed and bound in the United States of America.
ISBN: 978-0-9838302-5-2

Comments and corrections may be sent to comments@melioralaw.com. Although
the publisher has made every effort to ensure the accuracy of information contained
in this publication, it cannot assume liability for inadvertent errors.

Meliora Law LLC
19250 Stevens Creek Boulevard, Suite 100
Cupertino, CA 94015
www.melioralaw.com

PUBLISHER'S PREFACE

The information contained herein are current as received through March 1, 2012.

THE PUBLISHER

March 1, 2012

TABLE OF CONTENTS

Page

PUBLISHER'S PREFACE iii

PART I. DISTRICT COURT – GENERAL ORDERS

GENERAL ORDERS (SELECTED)

General Order No. 568 (Random Assignment of Criminal Cases)   3
General Order No. 541 (Delegation of Authority)   4
General Order No. 444 (Regulating Interpreters in U.S. Marshal's Holding
    Cells and Probation Interviews)   5
General Order No. 387-A (Amendment to Arbitration and
    Mediation Rules)   6
General Order No. 387 (Arbitration and Mediation Rules)   7

PART II. INDIVIDUAL JUDGES – PROCEDURES AND PRACTICES; CHAMBERS RULES AND STANDING ORDERS; SCHEDULING INFORMATION; AND CHAMBERS AND BIOGRAPHICAL INFORMATION

DISTRICT JUDGES

Anello, Michael M.
Chambers, Scheduling, and Biographical Information   19
Procedures and Practices
    Civil Chambers Rules   20
    Criminal Chambers Rules   22

Battaglia, Anthony J.
Chambers, Scheduling, and Biographical Information   23
Procedures and Practices
    Civil Case Procedures   24
    Criminal Case Chambers Rules   27
    Questions to be Asked on Voir Dire by the Court in a Civil Case   28
    Supplemental Questions to be Asked on Voir Dire by the Court
        in Section 1983 Cases   31

Bencivengo, Cathy Ann
Chambers, Scheduling, and Biographical Information   32

Benitez, Roger T.
Chambers, Scheduling, and Biographical Information 33

Brewster, Rudi M.
Chambers, Scheduling, and Biographical Information 34
Procedures and Practices
    Civil Pretrial and Trial Procedures 35

Burns, Larry Alan
Chambers, Scheduling, and Biographical Information 42
Procedures and Practices
    Standing Order in Civil Cases 43
    Standing Order in Criminal Cases 53

Gonzalez, Irma E.
Chambers, Scheduling, and Biographical Information 56

Hayes, William Q.
Chambers, Scheduling, and Biographical Information 57
Procedures and Practices
    Civil Pretrial and Trial Procedures 58
    Criminal Pretrial and Trial Procedures 62

Houston, John A.
Chambers, Scheduling, and Biographical Information 64

Huff, Marilyn L.
Chambers, Scheduling, and Biographical Information 65
Procedures and Practices 65

Lorenz, M. James
Chambers, Scheduling, and Biographical Information 66
Procedures and Practices
    Criminal Pretrial and Trial Procedures 67
    Standing Order for Civil Cases 70

Miller, Jeffrey T.
Chambers, Scheduling, and Biographical Information 74
Procedures and Practices
    Standing Rules for Civil Matters 75
    Standing Rules for Criminal Matters 80

Moskowitz, Barry Ted (Chief District Judge)
Chambers, Scheduling, and Biographical Information 83
Procedures and Practices
    Order Limiting Submission of Sentencing Materials 84

Sabraw, Dana M.
Chambers, Scheduling, and Biographical Information 85
Procedures and Practices
    Civil Pretrial and Trial Procedures 86
    Criminal Pretrial and Trial Procedures 93

Sammartino, Janis L.
Chambers, Scheduling, and Biographical Information 97

Thompson, Jr., Gordon
Chambers, Scheduling, and Biographical Information 98

Whelan, Thomas J.
Chambers, Scheduling, and Biographical Information 99
Procedures and Practices
    Chambers Rules for Civil Cases 100
    Chambers Rules for Criminal Cases 104

Magistrate Judges

Adler, Jan M.
Chambers, Scheduling, and Biographical Information 109
Procedures and Practices
    Chambers Rules 110
    Criminal Pretrial Procedures 113

Brooks, Ruben B.
Chambers, Scheduling, and Biographical Information 114

Dembin, Mitchell D.
Chambers, Scheduling, and Biographical Information 115
Procedures and Practices
    Chambers Rules – Civil Pretrial Procedures 116
    Chambers Rules – Criminal Pretrial Procedures 120

Gallo, William V.
Chambers, Scheduling, and Biographical Information 122
Procedures and Practices
    Chambers Rules for Civil Cases 123
    Criminal Pretrial Procedures 129

Lewis, Peter C.
Chambers, Scheduling, and Biographical Information 131

Major, Barbara Lynn
Chambers, Scheduling, and Biographical Information 132

McCurine, William Jr.
Chambers, Scheduling, and Biographical Information 133
Procedures and Practices
    Chambers Rules – Civil Pretrial Procedures 134
    Chambers Rules – Criminal Pretrial Procedures 137

Porter, Louisa S.
Chambers, Scheduling, and Biographical Information 138
Procedures and Practices
    Civil Discovery Conferences 139
    Protective Orders 141

Skomal, Bernard G.
Chambers, Scheduling, and Biographical Information 142
Procedures and Practices
    Chambers Rules 143
    Criminal Pretrial Procedures 148

Stormes, Nita L. (Presiding Magistrate Judge)
Chambers, Scheduling, and Biographical Information 149
Procedures and Practices
    Civil Case Procedures 150
    Criminal Pretrial Procedures 154

This page intentionally left blank.

This page intentionally left blank.

PART I

DISTRICT COURT
SELECTED GENERAL ORDERS

I. **General Orders**

A. *General Order No. 568 – Random Assignment of Criminal Cases*

GENERAL ORDER NO. 568

Random Assignment of Criminal Cases

The clerk of court will randomly assign a criminal action or proceeding to a judge pursuant to Criminal Local Rule 57.2(a), except the clerk will assign a related indictment to the judge who has a pending indictment or information as to the same defendant.

IT IS SO ORDERED.

DATED: May 28, 2008

B.   *General Order No. 541 – Delegation of Authority*

GENERAL ORDER NO. 541

Delegation of Authority

NOW, THEREFORE, IT IS ORDERED that absent an order to the contrary, any judge sitting in this District is designated to handle any matters requiring action on cases assigned to a judge who is unavailable.

The Court reserves the right to designate specifically for a particular case in the efficient administration of justice.

DATED: September 20, 2004

C. *General Order No. 444 – Regulating Interpreters in U.S. Marshal's Holding Cells and Probation Interviews*

GENERAL ORDER NO. 444

Regulating Interpreters in U.S. Marshal's Holding Cells and Probation Interviews

The court has received inquiry form the Marshal's Service and the Probation Department concerning persons who seek to act as defense interpreters of defendants in the court's holding cells or of defendants during interviews with probation officers. Specifically, the court has been informed that because there are no clear guidelines, family members or friends of a defendant have acted as interpreters, as well as persons with no documentation of their profession who claim to be interpreters. The court finds that standards must be set since both situations often involve highly sensitive information being exchanged between a defendant and his/her attorney or probation officer. Because the holding cells are small and the court is experiencing a large increase in criminal cases, interpreters are able to overhear conversations between lawyers and their clients, including the topic of cooperation with the government. Moreover, the court has mandated that if a defendant is cooperating, the Probation Officer must discuss the nature of the cooperation with the defendant. Hence, the court orders the following:

1. Only interpreters certified by the state of California or the federal government may be allowed to act as interpreters in the Marshal's holding cells or during probation interviews.

2. The court's supervising interpreter will maintain a list of certified interpreters who wish to interpret in the holding cells or for probation interviews, and will regularly provide a copy to the Marshal's Service and the Probation Department.

3. Any interpreter desiring to be placed on the list must provide a copy of his/her certification to the supervising interpreter for photocopying so that its validity may be verified.

4. If desired, an attorney may contact the supervising interpreter 24 hours in advance and he/she will provide an interpreter to assist in the holding cells, throughout the day at no cost.

5. Because of security concerns, no certified interpreter who is a family member or friend of a prisoner may interpret for him/her in holding cells or during probation interviews.

6. Because of security and confidentiality concerns, no certified interpreter who a) is residing with a person who is charged in a pending federal indictment, who is a federal prisoner or on federal supervision, or b) has an immediate family member (child, parent, spouse, sibling) in federal prison or show is on active federal supervision or is charged in a pending federal indictment may interpret in the holding cells or during probation interviews.

DATED: April 18, 1997

D. *General Order No. 387-A – Amendment to Arbitration and Mediation Rules*

GENERAL ORDER NO. 387-A

Arbitration and Mediation Rules

GOOD CAUSE APPEARING, the Arbitration and Mediation Rules are amended to add the following section:

Rule 600-8
MEDIATION PROCEDURE

(c) Confidentiality. This court, the mediator, all counsel and parties, and any other persons participating in the mediation process shall treat as confidential all written and oral communications made in connection with or during any mediation session. The court hereby extends to all such communications all the protection afforded by Federal Rule of Evidence 408 and by Federal Rule of Civil Procedure 68. In addition, unless otherwise stipulated by all parties and the mediator, the court hereby prohibits disclosure of any written or oral communication made by any party, counsel, mediator or other participant in connection with or during any mediation to anyone not involved in the litigation. Nor may such communication, absent stipulation by all parties and the mediator, be disclosed to the assigned trial judge or used for any purpose, including impeachment, in any pleading or future proceeding in court.

DATED: January 3, 2000

E. *General Order No. 387 – Arbitration and Mediation Rules*

GENERAL ORDER NO. 387

Arbitration and Mediation Rules

The attached Arbitration and Mediation Rules are approved and adopted by the court effective January 9, 1992.

DATED: January 9, 1992

TABLE OF RULES
VI. ARBITRATION AND MEDIATION

Rule 600-1. PURPOSE OF ARBITRATION AND MEDIATION

Rule 600-2. PRELIMINARY PROCEDURE
(a)   Initial AM Order
(b)   Discovery
(c)   Dispositive Motions

Rule 600-3. ARBITRATORS AND MEDIATORS
(a)   Approval
(b)   Eligibility
(c)   Oath or Affirmation

Rule 600-4. SELECTION OF THE ARBITRATOR OR MEDIATOR
(a)   Selection by Agreement
(b)   Selection by the Court
(c)   Disqualification
(d)   Hearing

Rule 600-5. ARBITRATION PROCEDURE
(a)   No *Ex Parte* Communication
(b)   Pre-Hearing Exchange of Information
(c)   Record and Use
(d)   Subpoenas
(e)   Testimony Under Oath or Affirmation
(f)   Conduct of Hearing
(g)   Evidence
(h)   Conclusion of Hearing
(i)   Sanctions for Failure to Proceed

Rule 600-6. ARBITRATION AWARD AND JUDGMENT
(a)   Issuance of Award
(b)   Award Procedure

Rule 600-7. MEDIATION PROCEDURE
(a)   No *Ex Parte* Communication
(b)   Pre-Hearing Exchange of Information
(c)   Attendance

     (d)   Record and Use

     (e)   Mediator's Suggestions

     (f)   Notice of Compliance

     (g)   Sanctions for Failure to Proceed

Rule 600-8. POST-HEARING PROCEEDINGS

     (a)   Return to Court

     (b)   Evidence from the Arbitration Hearing

Rule 600-1
PURPOSE OF ARBITRATION AND MEDIATION

    These rules govern references of selected actions to non binding arbitration and mediation. Their purpose is to provide for the speedy, fair, and economical resolution of controversies by informal procedures while preserving the right of all parties to a conventional trial.

Rule 600-2
PRELIMINARY PROCEDURE

    (a)   Initial AM Order. At the time of the ENE the court shall announce to the parties, and thereafter the clerk shall enter, in each case subject to mandatory arbitration or mediation, an initial AM order which:

    1.   refers the case for arbitration or mediation; and,

    2.   notifies the parties of their opportunity to select an agreed upon arbitrator. The parties may select an arbitrator from the list of arbitrators maintained by the court, or they may select any other person, whether or not an attorney, on the basis of that person's expertise or experience. To select an agreed upon arbitrator or mediator, the parties must, at the time of the ENE, announce the name of the arbitrator or mediator chosen and thereafter file with the court a stipulation identifying the arbitrator within three (3) days after the ENE.

    (b)   Discovery. Discovery shall proceed as in any other civil act ion.

    (c)   Dispositive Motions. In a case selected for mandatory arbitration or mediation, summary judgment and other dispositive motions will not be ruled upon by the court until the case has proceeded through an arbitration or mediation hearing and has returned to the court calendar.

Rule 600-3
ARBITRATORS AND MEDIATORS

    (a)   Approval. The court shall receive applications from attorneys who agree to serve as arbitrators or mediators without compensation. From time-to-time, the court will review the applications of attorneys for approval pursuant to section (b) of this rule. The court shall maintain a list of approved arbitrators and mediators, showing the name address, telephone number, and professional affiliation (if appropriate) of each. The court shall also maintain a file of resumes for the arbitrators and mediators, each resume to contain a short professional history of each.

    (b)   Eligibility. Any individual may be approved to serve as an arbitrator or mediator if the person:

1.   has been for at least five (5) years a member of the bar of the highest court of any state or the District of Columbia; and

2.   is a member of the bar of this court;

(c)   Oath or Affirmation. Each arbitrator shall take an oath or affirmation similar to that prescribed by 28 U.S.C. 5 453 before serving as an arbitrator or mediator. A written statement made under penalty of perjury and filed with the court will satisfy this

requirement.

Rule 600-4
SELECTION OF THE ARBITRATOR OR MEDIATOR

(a)   Selection by Agreement. If the parties select an agreed upon arbitrator or mediator at the time of the ENE and thereafter file with the court a timely stipulation pursuant to Rule 600-2 (a) 2, identifying an agreed upon arbitrator or mediator, the court shall thereupon appoint such person as the arbitrator or mediator and give notice of the appointment to the arbitrator or mediator and the parties.

(b)   Selection by the Court. If the parties fail to select an agreed upon arbitrator or mediator at the time of the ENE, the court shall, at the ENE, appoint an arbitrator or mediator to serve and shall thereafter notify each party and the selected arbitrator or mediator of the appointment.

(c)   Disqualification. On motion made to the court within five (5) days after the appointment described under section (b) of this rule, an arbitrator or mediator may be disqualified by the court for bias or prejudice as provided in 28 U.S.C. 5 144. Further, an arbitrator or mediator shall disqualify her or himself if he or she could be required to do so under 28 U.S.C. 5 455 if a District Judge or Magistrate Judge.

(d)   Hearing. Regardless of the manner by which selection is made, the arbitrator or mediator shall set a hearing at a time and place convenient to all, but, in any event, to be held within forty-five (45) days after the ENE conference. Absent written court order, based upon good cause, there will not be any extensions of the deadline within which the hearing is to be held. It is the policy of the court to discourage continuances and extensions of the hearing and related deadlines.

Rule 600-5
ARBITRATION PROCEDURE

(a)   No *Ex Parte* Communication. There shall be no *ex parte* communication between the arbitrator and any counsel or party on any matter touching the proceeding, except with regard to scheduling matters. Nothing in this rule prevents the arbitrator from discussing substantive issues in the case with all parties present or from assisting settlement negotiations between the parties at any time following appointment.

(b)   Pre-Hearing Exchange of Information. No later than ten (10) days prior to the hearing date, or at a time agreed upon among each of the parties and the arbitrator, each party shall serve on the arbitrator and other parties a statement which sets forth for such party the following information:

1.   identification of the issues to be determined;

2.　　identification of all witnesses to be called at the arbitration hearing except for impeachment witnesses; and

3.　　identification of all exhibits to be presented at the hearing except for impeachment.

Each party may, at the same time, serve a pre hearing brief. Statements and briefs served under this rule are not to be filed with the court.

(c)　　Record and use of information. No official record of the arbitration hearing will be made. All proceedings of the arbitration including any statement made by any party, attorney or other participant, shall, in all respects, be protected and not reported, recorded, placed in evidence, made known to the trial court or jury, or construed for any purpose as an admission against interest. No party shall be bound by anything done or said at the

arbitration unless a settlement is reached, in which event the agreement upon a settlement shall be reduced to writing and shall be binding upon all parties to that agreement. Nothing in this subsection shall preclude the parties from arranging for a reporter to be present for any arbitration which the parties stipulate will be binding.

(d)　　Subpoenas. Rule 45 of the Federal Rules of Civil Procedure shall apply to subpoenas for attendance of witnesses and the production of documentary evidence at an arbitration hearing under these rules.

(e)　　Testimony Under Oath or Affirmation. All witness shall testify under oath or affirmation administered by the arbitrator (who is designated a Master for this purpose only) or by any duly qualified person.

(f)　　Conduct of Hearing. At the opening of the arbitration hearing, the arbitrator shall make a written record of the place, time, and date of the hearing, and the presence of the parties and counsel. The arbitrator and the parties shall review the written statements concerning issues, witnesses, and exhibits served pursuant to section (b) of this rule. Plaintiff may then present its exhibits (copies only) and witnesses, who may be cross-examined. Defendant may then present its exhibits (copies only) and witnesses, who may be cross-examined. In the discretion of the arbitrator, this procedure may be varied.

(g)　　Evidence. The arbitrator shall weigh all evidence presented and assess its relevance and trustworthiness. The Federal Rules of Evidence shall not apply, except for rules applying to privilege.

(h)　　Conclusion of Hearing. When the parties state that they have no further exhibits or witnesses to offer, the arbitrator shall declare the hearing closed. Counsel may make oral argument, but the filing of post hearing briefs will ordinarily not be permitted. If the arbitrator decides to accept briefs, such briefs must be served upon the arbitrator and other parties as determined by the arbitrator.

(i)　　Sanctions for Failure to Proceed. For any failure of a party or its counsel to participate or proceed in good faith in accordance with these rules, the Court may impose sanctions.

Rule 600-6
ARBITRATION AWARD AND JUDGMENT

(a)   Issuance of Award. The arbitrator shall issue the award either at the conclusion of the hearing or within five (5) court days of the date of the closing of the hearing or the receipt of post hearing briefs, whichever is later. If not announced at the hearing, the arbitrator shall send a copy of the award to the parties.

(b)   Award Procedure. The award shall dispose of all monetary claims presented to the arbitrator and shall, if not announced orally at the time of the hearing, be signed by the arbitrator. The arbitrator is not required to issue an opinion explaining the award.

Rule 600-7
MEDIATION PROCEDURE

(a)   No *Ex Parte* Communication. Prior to the proceeding, there shall be no *ex parte* communication between the mediator and any counsel or party on any matter touching the proceeding, except with regard to scheduling matters. Nothing in this rule prevents the mediator from discussing substantive issues in the case with all parties present or from assisting settlement negotiations between the parties at any time following the opening of the

mediation conference.

(b)   Pre-Hearing Exchange of Information. No later than ten (10) days prior to the hearing date, or at a time agreed upon among each of the parties and mediator, each party shall serve on the mediator and other parties a statement which sets forth for such party a concise statement of contentions regarding both liability and damages. Statements served under this rule are not to be filed with the court.

(c)   Attendance. The attorney and the clients, unless excused by the mediator, shall personally attend the mediation conference and any adjourned sessions. The attorney shall be prepared to discuss all liability and damage issues as well as the position of the client relative to settlement. Parties whose defense is provided by a liability insurance company, and a representative of the insurer of said parties, shall attend and shall be empowered to bind the insurer to a settlement if a settlement can be reached within the limits of the policy in question.

(d)   Record and use of information. All proceedings of the mediation conference, including any statement made by any party, attorney or other participant, shall, in all respects, be protected and not reported, recorded, placed in evidence, made known to the trial court or jury, or construed for any purpose as an admission against interest. No party shall be bound by anything done or said at the conference unless a settlement is reached, in which event the agreement upon a settlement shall be reduced to writing and shall be binding upon all parties to that agreement.

(e)   Mediator's suggestions. If the mediator makes any oral or written suggestion as to the advisability of a change in any party's position with respect to settlement, the attorney for that party shall promptly transmit that suggestion to the client. The mediator is under no obligation to make any written comments or recommendations but may, in his or her discretion, provide the attorneys with a written settlement recommendation memorandum. No copy of any such memorandum shall be filed with the court or made available in whole or in part, directly or indirectly, either to the court or the jury.

(f)   Notice of Compliance or noncompliance. If no settlement results from the mediation, the mediator shall promptly file with the court a statement showing that there has been compliance or noncompliance with the settlement and mediation requirements of this Rule but that no settlement has been reached. The case will then be placed back on the normal trial calendar schedule.

(g)   Sanctions for Failure to Proceed. For any failure of a party, its representative or its counsel to participator proceed in good faith in accordance with these rules, the Court may impose sanctions.

Rule 600-8
POST HEARING PROCEEDINGS

(a)   Return t o Court. Unless the case settles, the action shall be returned to the court's normal trial calendar schedule.

The Magistrate Judge assigned to the case may use the results of the arbitration or mediation for case management or settlement purposes.

(b)   Evidence From the Arbitration Hearing or Mediation Conference. At the trial of the action, the court shall not admit evidence that there has been an arbitration proceeding or mediation conference or result of either.

This page intentionally left blank.

This page intentionally left blank.

PART II

INDIVIDUAL JUDGES
PROCEDURES AND PRACTICES
CHAMBERS RULES
STANDING ORDERS
SCHEDULING INFORMATION
CHAMBERS AND BIOGRAPHICAL INFORMATION

DISTRICT JUDGES

Hon. Michael M. Anello
District Judge

Chambers Information

U.S. District Court, Southern District of California
Courtroom 5, 3rd Floor
940 Front Street
San Diego, CA 92101

Scheduling Information

Courtroom Deputy: (619) 557-2921

Criminal Matters	Mondays at 9:00 a.m. and 2:00 p.m.

Biographical Information

Born 1943 in Miami, FL

Federal Judicial Service:

- Judge, U. S. District Court, Southern District of California
- Nominated by George W. Bush on April 30, 2008, to a seat vacated by Napoleon A. Jones; Confirmed by the Senate on September 26, 2008, and received commission on October 10, 2008.

Education:

- Bowdoin College, B.A., 1965
- Georgetown University Law Center, J.D., 1968

Professional Career:

- United States Marine Corps, Active Duty, 1968-1972
- United States Marine Corps Reserve, 1973-1990
- Deputy City Attorney, San Diego City Attorney's Office, California, 1972-1973
- Private Practice, San Diego, California, 1973-1998
- Judge, San Diego Superior Court, 1998-2008

I.   **Judge Anello's Procedures and Practices**
        A.   *Civil Chambers Rules*

Civil Chambers Rules of Judge Michael M. Anello

Unless otherwise ordered, matters before Judge Anello shall be conducted in accordance with the rules stated below. These rules do not alter the requirements of this Court's Civil Local Rules or the Federal Rules of Civil Procedure.

I.   MOTION PRACTICE GENERALLY

All dates for motion hearings must be obtained by contacting Chambers and speaking with the law clerk assigned to the case. After obtaining a hearing date from the law clerk, the moving party must file the motion within 3 court days. Parties who fail to file their papers within 3 court days of obtaining the hearing date forfeit the assigned hearing date.

The Court in its discretion may resolve motions on the papers, in accordance with Civil Local Rule 7.1.d.1. If the moving party does not wish to have oral argument, they should include "No Oral Argument Requested" in the caption on the front of their papers, directly below the hearing date. The Court shall consider requests regarding oral argument and accommodate a request if suitable. If the Court determines oral argument is necessary, the parties should plan to appear in person on the date and at the time of the scheduled motion hearing. If the Court decides to take the motion under submission on the papers, a minute order shall be issued on the docket of the case no later than 2 court days prior to the scheduled hearing date notifying the parties that no appearances are required. Thereafter, the Court shall take the hearing off calendar and issue a written ruling on the motion in due course.

II.   MOTIONS FOR SUMMARY JUDGMENT

All motions for summary judgment shall be accompanied by a separate statement of undisputed material facts. If the moving party fails to submit a separate statement of undisputed material facts with the moving papers, the Court may reject the filing as discrepant for failing to comply with this Chambers requirement. Any opposition to a summary judgment motion shall include a response to the separate statement of undisputed material facts. In addition, any evidentiary and procedural objections to the motion for summary judgment must be contained within the opposition brief. Similarly, the moving party must include any evidentiary and procedural objections to the opposition brief in its reply brief. Any separately filed objections shall be stricken and will not be considered by the Court.

III.   TEMPORARY RESTRAINING ORDERS

All motions for temporary restraining orders shall be briefed. While temporary restraining orders may be heard in true *ex parte* fashion (i.e., without notice to an opposing party), the Court will do so only in extraordinary circumstances. The Court's strong preference is for the opposing party to be served and afforded a reasonable opportunity to file an opposition. In appropriate cases, the Court may issue a limited restraining order to preserve evidence pending further briefing.

IV.   PROPOSED ORDERS AND JOINT MOTIONS

Proposed orders should be submitted simultaneously with all motions, except motions that are fully-noticed and set for hearing at least 28 days beyond the date of filing. In accordance with Section 2(h) of the Electronic Case Filing Administrative Policies and Procedures Manual (available at http://www.casd.uscourts.gov/cmecf/pdf/CASDPolicies.pdf), counsel should email proposed orders directly to Judge Anello's official email address, which is efile_anello@casd.uscourts.gov.

V.   EX PARTE MOTIONS

Before filing any *ex parte* motion, counsel shall contact the opposing party to meet and confer regarding the subject of the *ex parte* motion. All *ex parte* motions shall be accompanied by a declaration from counsel documenting (1) efforts to contact opposing counsel, (2) counsel's meet and confer efforts, and (3) opposing counsel's position regarding the *ex parte* motion. Any *ex parte* motion filed with the Court shall be served on opposing counsel via facsimile, electronic mail with return receipt requested, or overnight mail. *Ex parte* motions that are not opposed within **one Court day** shall be considered unopposed and may be granted on that ground.

VI.   MOTIONS IN LIMINE

Motions in limine shall be heard at the final pretrial conference.[1] Motions in limine shall be filed at least 28 days before the final pretrial conference; oppositions to motions in limine shall be filed at least 14 days before the final pretrial conference. No reply briefs will be accepted.

Each side that intends to file motions in limine is limited to a maximum of 10 motions in limine. Each side's in limine motions must be filed as a single brief, and shall not exceed 25 pages in length.

The opposing side shall file a single brief in opposition to the motions in limine, not to exceed 20 pages in length.

As the language above indicates, if the case involves multiple plaintiffs or multiple defendants, only one motion in limine brief *per side* will be accepted. Unless the parties obtain leave of Court to exceed the limitations contained herein prior to filing, multiple filings and filings that exceed the page limitations will be stricken. The Court makes every effort to provide tentative rulings on the motions in limine prior to the final pretrial conference and will entertain oral argument on the motions at the final pretrial conference.

VII.   COURTESY COPIES

Courtesy copies of filings that exceed 20 pages in length shall be submitted directly to Chambers as soon as practicable after filing. This includes multiple filings in a single court day that together exceed 20 pages in length (i.e., moving papers consisting of a Notice of Motion (3 pages), a Memorandum of Points and Authorities (12 pages), an Exhibit (10 pages), and a Certificate of Service (2 pages)). Please consult the Electronic Case Filing Administrative Policies and Procedures Manual for further information regarding the courtesy copy requirement.

---

[1]   Please note that *Daubert* motions must be filed prior to the dispositive motions deadline set by the operative scheduling/case management order.

B. *Criminal Chambers Rules*

CRIMINAL CHAMBERS RULES

All matters before Judge Anello shall be conducted in accordance with the following practices. Except as otherwise provided herein, or as specifically ordered by the Court, all parties are expected to comply strictly with the Local Rules of the Southern District of California and the Federal Rules of Criminal Procedure.

CALENDAR

Criminal matters are heard on Mondays at 9:00 a.m. and 2:00 p.m., unless otherwise scheduled by the Court. A party seeking a continuance of a hearing must notify Judge Anello's Courtroom Deputy at the earliest possible time. Please be advised that continuance requests made less than three (3) court days prior to a hearing may not result in the hearing being taken off calendar, and any such request will have to be renewed on the record during the scheduled hearing.

COURTESY COPIES

Unless otherwise ordered by the Court, for any document which exceeds **20** pages in length (including attachments and exhibits), the filing party must deliver a courtesy copy directly to Chambers within 24 hours after filing. Please be advised that expeditious delivery is particularly important when a party has filed a lengthy sentencing document less than five (5) court days prior the scheduled sentencing hearing.

SENTENCING SUMMARY CHARTS

All counsel shall adhere strictly to Criminal Local Rule 32.1(a)(9), which provides that completed sentencing summary charts must be filed no later than seven (7) days prior to a scheduled sentencing hearing.

TRIAL PROCEDURES

A. <u>Trial Briefs:</u> The parties shall file trial briefs five (5) days prior to the date of trial. The parties should consult Criminal Local Rule 23.1 regarding proper form and content.

B. <u>Proposed Jury Instructions:</u> The parties shall file proposed jury instructions five (5) days prior to the date of trial, unless otherwise ordered by the Court. The Court prefers to use the Model Jury Instructions for the Ninth Circuit whenever possible. The parties should consult Criminal Local Rule 30.1 regarding proper form and content.

C. <u>Witness and Exhibit Lists:</u> The parties shall file witness and exhibit lists five (5) days prior to the date of the trial, unless otherwise ordered by the Court.

D. Trial Schedule: In general, criminal trials are scheduled from 9:00 a.m. to 4:30 p.m., beginning on Tuesdays, including a lunch recess from approximately 12:00 noon to 1:30 p.m. and morning and afternoon breaks. The Court will notify the parties of deviations from this schedule, and when possible will attempt to accommodate jurors, witnesses, and counsel, should conflicts arise.

Hon. Anthony J. Battaglia
District Judge

Chambers Information
U.S. District Court, Southern District of California
Courtroom 12, 2nd Floor
940 Front Street
San Diego, CA 92101

Scheduling Information
Courtroom Deputy: (619) 557-6423

Criminal Matters	Fridays at 9:00 a.m.

Biographical Information
Born 1949 in San Diego, CA

Federal Judicial Service:
- Judge, U. S. District Court, Southern District of California
- Nominated by Barack Obama on January 5, 2011, to a seat vacated by M. James Lorenz; Confirmed by the Senate on March 7, 2011, and received commission on March 9, 2011. U.S. Magistrate Judge, U.S. District Court, Southern District of California, 1993-2011

Education:
- United States International University, B.A., 1971
- California Western School of Law, J.D., 1974

Professional Career:
- Private practice, San Diego, California, 1974-1993

I.   **Judge Battaglia's Procedures and Practices**
        A.   Civil Case Procedures

CIVIL CASE PROCEDURES

Please Note: The Court provides this information for general guidance to counsel. However, the Court may vary these procedures as appropriate in any case.

Communications With Chambers

A. **Letters or e:mails.** Letters or e:mails to chambers are prohibited unless specifically requested by the Court. If letters or e:mails are requested, copies of the same must be simultaneously delivered to all counsel. Copies of correspondence between counsel must *not* be sent to the Court unless specifically requested by the Court.

B. **Faxes.** Faxes to chambers are prohibited unless specifically requested by the Court. If faxes are requested, copies of the must shall be simultaneously delivered to all counsel.

C. **Telephone Calls.** Telephone calls to chambers are permitted only for matters such as scheduling and calendaring. Court personnel are prohibited from giving legal advice or discussing the merits of a case. When calling chambers, be prepared to identify your case as odd or even based on the last digit of the case number so your call can be directed to the appropriate law clerk. Call the chambers at 619-557-3446 and address your inquiries to the law clerk. *Only counsel* with knowledge of the case may contact chambers.

D. **Document submissions.** Please refer to the Local Rules for a complete list of deadlines and compliance requirements. The Electronic Case Filing Administrative Policies & Procedures Manual can be found on the Court's website. Courtesy copies of e-filed documents longer than *20 pages*, including exhibits, must be submitted to chambers. Failure to submit courtesy copies, may result in a continuance of the hearing.

Noticed Motions

A. **Hearing Dates.** Counsel shall obtain all hearing dates from the appropriate law clerk before filing moving papers. Moving papers **MUST** be filed and served *the same day* of obtaining a motion hearing date from chambers. Moving papers include, (1) the motion, (2) opposition and (3) reply. **Objections relating to the motion briefing should be set forth in the parties opposition or reply. The parties must obtain leave of Court before filing any sur-replies or a separate set of objections relating to the motion briefing.**

B. **Oral argument.** Although the Court often decides motions based on the papers submitted by the parties, it is the Court's policy to schedule oral argument for dispositive motions or when all counsel request oral argument. Counsel will be notified by the law clerk assigned to the case once the decision is made as to whether oral argument is needed to assist in deciding a given motion.

C. **Continuances.** Parties requesting a continuance of any conference, scheduled motion, hearing date, deadline, briefing schedule, or other procedural changes, shall meet and confer prior to contacting the Court. If the parties reach an agreement, they shall e-file a joint motion with a detailed declaration of the reason for the requested continuance or extension of time. They shall also e-mail a proposed order, **preferably in Wordperfect**, or Word format to efile_battaglia@casd.uscourts.gov. detailing the current date scheduled and the new date proposed. Please refer to the Case Filing Administrative Policies and Procedures Manual located on the Court's website with regard to CM/ECF filings. If the parties are unable to reach an agreement, the requesting party shall file an ex parte motion satisfying the applicable legal standard, with a particular focus on the diligence of the party seeking delay and any prejudice that may result therefrom. In addition, the ex parte shall state (1) the original date, (2) the number of previous continuances and requests, (3) whether previous requests were granted or denied and (4) opposing counsel's position with regard to their opposition.

D. **Proposed Orders.** Proposed orders must be submitted simultaneously with the filing of all joint motions or ex parte motions. The proposed order should be e:mailed to efile_battaglia@casd.uscourts.gov, preferably in Wordperfect, or Word format.

E. **Sur-Replies.** Sur-replies shall **not** be filed unless leave of Court has been granted.

F. **Separate Statements of Fact.** Separate Statements of Fact shall **not** be filed unless leave of Court has been granted pursuant to Civ. Local Rule 7.1.f.1.

G. Motions in Limine.

1. Motions in Limine will typically be heard in advance of the first day of trial. Each side is allowed a maximum of five (5) motions in limine. Each motion and each opposition thereto are limited to ten (10) pages in length. Attachments are also limited to a maximum of ten (10) pages for any motion or opposition.

2. Prior to filing motions in limine, counsel must meet and confer and discuss their intended motions, and attempt to resolve those issues and enter into stipulations, as appropriate.

3. Counsel must confirm their good faith attempt to resolve the issues through the meet and confer process in their motion papers.

4. Motions in limine must be limited in scope to evidentiary issues where attempts to "unring the bell" would be unduly prejudicial or futile. Motions for judgment on the pleadings, summary judgment or summary adjudication, Daubert, leave to amend or bifurcation are not in limine motions within the scope of this order.

5. The Court will grant motions to exclude witnesses, to allow electronic equipment, and to shackle inmate civil litigants on oral motion at or before trial outside of the five (5) motion limit.

Ex Parte Proceedings

Appropriate *ex parte* motions may be made at any time after first contacting the law clerk, but must ultimately be filed electronically on ECF. Before filing any *ex parte* motion, counsel shall contact the opposing party to meet and confer regarding the subject of the *ex parte* motion. All *ex parte* motions shall be accompanied by a declaration from counsel documenting (1) efforts to contact opposing counsel, (2) counsel's meet and confer efforts, and (3) opposing counsel's position regarding the *ex parte* motion. Any *ex parte* motion filed with the Court shall be served on opposing counsel via facsimile, electronic mail with return receipt requested, or overnight mail.

After service of the *ex parte* motion, opposing counsel will ordinarily be given until 5:00 p.m. On the next business day to respond. If more time is needed, opposing counsel must call the law clerk to modify the schedule. *Ex parte* motions that are not opposed, shall be considered unopposed and *may* be granted on that ground. After receipt, moving and opposing *ex parte* papers will be reviewed and a decision will be made without a hearing. If the Court requires a hearing, the parties will be contacted to set a date and time.

Seeking Leave to File Documents Under Seal

There is a presumptive right of public access to court records based upon common law and first amendment grounds.[1] Even where a public right of access exists, such access may be denied by the court in order to protect sensitive personal or confidential information.[2] The Court may seal documents to protect sensitive information, however, the documents to be filed under seal will be limited by the Court to <u>only those documents, or portions thereof, necessary to protect such sensitive information</u>.

Parties seeking a sealing order must provide the Court with: 1) a specific description of particular documents or categories of documents they need to protect; and 2) affidavits showing good cause to protect those documents from disclosure. Where good cause is shown for a protective order, the court must balance the potential harm to the moving party's interests against the public's right to access the court files. Any protective order must be narrowly drawn to reflect that balance. Any member of the public may challenge the sealing of any particular document. *See Citizens First Nat'l Bank of Princeton v. Cincinnati Ins. Co.*, 178 F.3d 943, 944-45 (7th Cir. 1999).

Temporary Restraining Orders

All motions for temporary restraining orders shall be briefed. While temporary restraining orders may be heard ex parte, the Court will do so only in extraordinary circumstances. The Court's strong preference is for the opposing party to be served and afforded a reasonable opportunity to file an opposition. In appropriate cases, the Court may issue a limited restraining order to preserve evidence pending further briefing.

---

[1] *See Nixon v. Warner Comm., Inc.*, 435 U.S. 589, 597 (1978); *Globe Newspaper Co. v. Superior Court for Norfolk County*, 457 U.S. 596, 603 (1982); *Phillips ex rel. Estates of Byrd v. General Motors Corp.*, 307 F.3d 1206, 1212 (9th Cir. 2002).

[2] Although courts may be more likely to order the protection of the information listed in Rule 26(c)(7) of the Federal Rules of Civil Procedure, courts have consistently prevented disclosure of many types of information, such as letters protected under attorney-client privilege which revealed the weaknesses in a party's position and was inadvertently sent to the opposing side, *see KL Group v. Case, Kay, and Lynch*, 829 F.2d 909, 917-19 (9th Cir.1987); medical and psychiatric records confidential under state law, *see Pearson v. Miller*, 211 F.3d 57, 62-64 (3d Cir.2000); and federal and grand jury secrecy provisions, *see Krause v. Rhodes*, 671 F.2d 212, 216 (6th Cir.1982). Most significantly, courts have granted protective orders to protect confidential settlement agreements. *See Hasbrouck v. BankAmerica Housing Serv.*, 187 F.R.D. 453, 455 (N.D.N.Y.1999); *Kalinauskas v. Wong*, 151 F.R.D. 363, 365-67 (D. Nev.1993).

B.   *Criminal Case Chambers Rules*

CRIMINAL CASE CHAMBERS RULES

All matters before Judge Battaglia shall be conducted in accordance with the following practices. Except as otherwise provided herein, or as specifically ordered by the Court, all parties are expected to comply strictly with the Local Rules of the Southern District of California and the Federal Rules of Criminal Procedure.

CALENDAR

Criminal matters are heard on Fridays at 9:00 a.m., unless otherwise scheduled by the Court. A party seeking a continuance of a hearing must notify Judge Battaglia's Courtroom Deputy at the earliest possible time. Please be advised that continuance requests made less than three (3) court days prior to a hearing may not result in the hearing being taken off calendar, and any such request will have to be renewed on the record during the scheduled hearing.

BAIL MATTERS

All bail matters are referred to the Magistrate Judges of this Court for handling.

PRETRIAL MOTIONS

Magistrate judges will schedule the motion hearing/trial setting on the Friday calendar.

Applications for an order shortening time are disfavored and must be supported by a nonconclusory affidavit signed by counsel setting forth facts establishing specific good cause.

Criminal motions requiring a predicate factual finding shall be supported by declaration(s). See Crim. L.R. 47.1.g.1. The Court need not grant an evidentiary hearing where either party fails to properly support its motion or opposition.

COURTESY COPIES

Unless otherwise ordered by the Court, for any document which exceeds 20 pages in length (including attachments and exhibits), the filing party must deliver a courtesy copy directly to chambers within 24 hours after filing. Please be advised that expeditious delivery is particularly important when a party has filed a lengthy sentencing document less than five (5) court days prior the scheduled sentencing hearing.

SENTENCING SUMMARY CHARTS

All counsel shall adhere strictly to Criminal Local Rule 32.1(a)(9), which provides that completed sentencing summary charts must be filed no later than **seven (7) days prior** to a scheduled sentencing hearing.

C. *Questions to be Asked on Voir Dire by the Court in a Civil Case*

IN THE UNITED STATES DISTICT COURT
FOR THE SOUTHERN DISTRICT OF CALIFORNIA

Plaintiff(s), v. Defendant(s).	) Civil No. _____)) **QUESTIONS TO BE ASKED ON**) **VOIR DIRE BY THE COURT IN A**) **CIVIL CASE. BRACKETED**) **QUESTIONS ARE ONLY ASKED**) **WHERE APPROPRIATE TO THE**) **CASE.**

1.   I am now going to question the prospective jurors concerning their qualifications to serve as jurors in this case.

2.   In the trial of this case, the parties are entitled to have a fair, unbiased and unprejudiced jury. If there is any reason why any of you might be biased or prejudiced in any way, you must disclose such reason when you are asked to do so. It is your duty to make this disclosure.

3.   This trial will likely take ____ or _____ days to complete, but it may take longer. Will any of you find it difficult or impossible to participate for this period of time?

4.   The nature of this case is as follows:

5.   Have any of you heard of, or have any knowledge of, the facts of events in this case?

6.   Do any of you believe that a case of this nature should not be brought to court for determination by a jury?

7.   The parties of this case and their respective attorneys are:

8.   During the trial of this case, the following witnesses may be called to testify on behalf of the parties. These witnesses are:

9.   Have any of you heard of or been otherwise acquainted with, related to, done business with, been employed by or had any dealings with any of the parties, attorneys or witnesses just named? The parties are not required and might not wish to call on these witnesses, and they may later find it necessary to call other witnesses.

10.   Do any of you have any belief or feeling toward any of the parties, attorneys or witnesses that might be regarded as a bias or prejudice for or against any of them? Do you have any interest, financial or otherwise, in the outcome of this case?

11.   Have any of you, or any member of your family or close friends, to your knowledge, ever filed an action against anyone, or presented a claim against anyone [including any of the parties in this case], in any civil case, excluding a domestic relations case. If so, did the matter terminate satisfactorily so far as you were concerned?

12.   Has anyone ever filed an action against any of you, or presented a claim

against any of you, or to your knowledge, against any member of your family or close friends? (If so, did the matter terminate satisfactorily so far as you were concerned?)

13. It may appear that one or more of the parties, attorneys, or witnesses come from a particular national, racial or religious group or may have a life style different than your own. Would this in any way affect your judgment or the weight and credibility you would give to their testimony?

14. Have any of you, or any member of your family or close friends, had any experience or special training in: (As appropriate to the case-law enforcement, accident reconstruction, engineering, investigations, medicine, psychology, the law, correctional institutions or claims adjusting)?

15. You may be called upon in this case to award monetary damages for personal injury, pain and suffering or emotional distress. Do any of you have any religious or other belief that pain and suffering or emotional distress are not real or any belief that would prevent you from awarding damages for pain and suffering or emotional distress if liability for them is established?

16. You may be called upon in this case to award punitive damages. The purpose of punitive damages are to punish a party and to deter that party and others from committing similar acts in the future. Do any of you have any religious or other belief that would prevent you from awarding punitive damages if liability for them is established.

17. "Plaintiff," is claiming injuries including "state injuries." Have any of you, or any member of your family or close friends, to your knowledge, suffer similar injuries? Have you or they, to your knowledge, suffered from similar injuries in the past? If so, would that fact affect your point of view in this case to the extent that you might not be able to render a completely fair and impartial verdict?

18. It would be natural for you to deeply sympathize with anyone who has received personal injuries or has suffered emotional distress. However, will you keep any such feelings of sympathy from interfering with your duty to render a just and impartial verdict based solely upon the law and evidence in this case?

19. Do any of you have any opinions of the amount of damages to be awarded in cases of this sort, such that there are limits in your mind that you would not go above or below, even though the law provided for a greater or lesser amount of damages?

20. If you or a member of your family were a party to this case or one like it – on either side - would you be willing to have your case tried, or theirs, by people in the same frame of mind as you are now?

21. It is important that I have your assurance that you will, without reservation, follow my instructions and rulings on the law and will apply that law to this case. To put it somewhat differently, whether you approve or disapprove of the Court's rulings or instructions, it is your solemn duty to accept, as correct, these statements of the law. You may not substitute your own idea of what you think the law ought to be. Will all of you follow the law as given to you by me in this case?

22. Do you realize your function is to decide the facts and then I will decide the law?

23.   Would you give both parties the benefit of your own individual opinion of this case?

24.   The evidence will be presented over the next several days. The plaintiff goes first, and the defendant goes second. Will you keep an open mind about what the verdict should be until after you have gone to the jury room to decide the case and you and your fellow jurors have discussed the evidence?

25.   Will you resolve this based on your own independent judgment, and will any verdict you return to the court truly reflect your own mind on the case?

26.   Would you use the same common sense you use in the conduct of your own affairs to reach a decision in this case?

27.   Would you decide the case without sympathy or prejudice?

28.   Do you think you can give each side a full and fair hearing, regardless of the eventual result that occurs?

29.   Do you know of any reason, or has anything occurred during this question period, that might make you doubtful that you would be a completely fair and impartial juror in this case? If there is, it is your duty to disclose the reason at this time.

30.   Each of you should now answer the questions on the paper before you as to your name, where you live, your marital status, whether married, single, widowed or divorced, the number and ages of your children, if any, your occupation, and the name of your present employer, if any, as well as the occupations and employers of your spouse or children, previous military service and previous jury service. Please begin with juror number one.

D. _Supplemental Questions to be Asked on Voir Dire by the Court in Section 1983 Cases_

IN THE UNITED STATES DISTICT COURT
FOR THE SOUTHERN DISTRICT OF CALIFORNIA

Plaintiff(s),	) Civil No. _____
v.	)
	) **SUPPLEMENTAL QUESTIONS TO**
	) **BE ASKED ON VOIR DIRE BY THE**
Defendant(s).	) **COURT IN § 1983 CASES.**
	) **BRACKETED QUESTIONS ARE**
	ONLY ASKED WHERE
	APPROPRIATE TO A PARTICULAR
	CASE.

A.   Do you have any opinions or beliefs regarding law enforcement officers, the California Department of Corrections, [or other state agency] or the fact that plaintiff is [or was at the time of the claims raised in this case] a prison inmate [and for standard security reasons will be guarded and shackled during the trial], that you think may influence your role as an impartial juror? If so, please describe those opinions or beliefs, and how you believe they may influence you as a juror.

B.   Have you or any of your family members or close friends ever been the victim of a crime? If so, will that affect your ability to serve as a fair and impartial juror?

C.   Have you or a close friend or family member ever been arrested or interviewed by a law enforcement officer? If so, will that affect your ability to serve as a fair and impartial juror?

D.   Have you or any of your family members or close friends ever been in jail or prison? If so, will that affect your ability to serve as a fair and impartial juror?

E.   With the fact that the defendants are represented by the California State Attorney General's Office [City Attorney, County Counsel], affect your ability to serve as a fair and impartial juror?

Hon. Cathy Ann Bencivengo
District Judge

Chambers Information
U.S. District Court, Southern District of California
Courtroom 2, 4th Floor
940 Front Street
San Diego, CA 92101

Scheduling Information
Courtroom Deputy: (619) 557-6901

Biographical Information
Born 1958 in Teaneck, NJ

Federal Judicial Service:
- Judge, U.S. District Court, Southern District of California
- Nominated by Barack Obama on May 11, 2011, to a seat vacated by Jeffrey T. Miller. Confirmed by the Senate on February 9, 2012, and received commission on February 10, 2012.
- U.S. Magistrate Judge, U.S. District Court, Southern District of California, 2005-2012

Education:
- Rutgers University, B.A., 1980
- Rutgers University, M.A., 1981
- University of Michigan Law School, J.D., 1988

Professional Career:
- Private practice, San Diego, California, 1988-2005

Hon. Roger T. Benitez
District Judge

Chambers Information
U.S. District Court, Southern District of California
Courtroom 3, 4th Floor
940 Front Street
San Diego, CA 92101

Scheduling Information
Courtroom Deputy: (619) 557-6422

Biographical Information
Born 1950 in Havana, Cuba

Federal Judicial Service:
- Judge, U. S. District Court, Southern District of California
- Nominated by George W. Bush on May 1, 2003, to a new seat created by 116 Stat. 1758;
Confirmed by the Senate on June 17, 2004, and received commission on June 21, 2004.
- U.S. Magistrate Judge, U.S. District Court for the Southern District of California, 2001-2004

Education:
- Imperial Valley College, A.A., 1971
- San Diego State University, B.A., 1974
- Western State University, J.D., 1978

Professional Career:
- Private practice, Imperial County, California, 1978-1997
- Judge, State of California Superior Court, 1997-2001
- Instructor, Imperial Valley College, 1998-1999

Hon. Rudi M. Brewster
District Judge

Chambers Information
U.S. District Court, Southern District of California
Courtroom 2, 4th Floor
940 Front Street
San Diego, CA 92101

Scheduling Information
Courtroom Deputy: (619) 557-6419

Biographical Information
Born 1932 in Sioux Falls, SD

Federal Judicial Service:
- Judge, U. S. District Court, Southern District of California
- Nominated by Ronald Reagan on May 24, 1984, to a seat vacated by Howard B. Turrentine; Confirmed by the Senate on June 15, 1984, and received commission on June 15, 1984. Assumed senior status on July 1, 1998.

Education:
- Princeton University, B.A., 1954
- Stanford Law School, J.D., 1960

Professional Career:
- U.S. Navy, 1954-1957
- U.S. Naval Reserve, 1957-1981
- Private Practice, San Diego, California, 1960-1984

I.   **Judge Brewster's Procedures and Practices**
    A.   *Civil Pretrial and Trial Procedures*

CIVIL PRETRIAL AND TRIAL PROCEDURES

Please note: The Court provides this information for general guidance to counsel. However, the Court may vary these procedures as appropriate in any case.

GENERAL DECORUM

Please be on time for each court session. Trial engagements take precedence over any other business. If you have matters in any other courtroom, arrange in advance for the handling of such matters by you or have an associate handle them for you.

The Court uses a sound recording system to create the official record for all proceedings. Therefore, whenever speaking, counsel must use a microphone so that the Court's electronic recording system will contain a complete record. If counsel moves away from the lectern, counsel must speak into a microphone.

All persons, whether observers, witnesses, lawyers, or clients, must maintain proper decorum while in Court. Counsel shall rise (being cognizant of the need to speak into a microphone) when addressing the Court, examining a witness, and in jury cases when the jury enters or leaves the courtroom. When addressing the Court, counsel should use "Your Honor," as opposed to "Judge." Counsel should only address the Court--not the law clerk, courtroom deputy, court reporter, or opposing counsel.

Pursuant to Civil Local Rule 83.4, lawyers must behave in a professional manner. Specifically, lawyers must:

(1)   Be courteous and civil in all communications, oral and written.

(2)   Be a vigorous and zealous advocate on behalf of a client without acting in a manner detrimental to the proper functioning of the judicial system.

(3)   Attempt to resolve litigation consistent with the interest of his/her client.

(4)   Attempt to informally resolve disputes with opposing counsel.

(5)   Agree to reasonable scheduling changes, requests for extensions of time and waivers of procedural formalities, if the legitimate interest of a client will not be adversely affected.

(6)   Communicate with opposing counsel in an attempt to establish a discovery plan and voluntary exchange of information.

(7)   When possible, confer with opposing counsel before scheduling or rescheduling hearings, depositions, and meetings and notify all parties and the Court as early as possible when hearings or depositions must be canceled.

Parties are reminded of their responsibility to ensure that papers filed with the Court are in conformance with the Local Rules, i.e., double spaced on one side, in 10-point Courier font or 12-point Times New Roman font, and within the page requirements.

ORDERS

Orders that are prepared for the Court should not be prepared on counsel's letterhead. The Court will usually prepare its own written order ruling on civil motions.

STIPULATIONS

Stipulations agreed upon during trial need not be signed by the Court. However, counsel should meet and confer outside the presence of the jury before presenting a stipulation to the Court.

Any stipulation for which the parties seek Court approval shall include the language "And Order Thereon" in both the title of the stipulation and in the body of the document.

SETTLEMENT

If the parties settle a case, counsel should immediately notify a law clerk of the settlement. Within twenty-eight (28) days of notification, the parties shall file a "Joint Stipulation And Order Thereon" for dismissal of the case.

INITIAL STATUS CONFERENCE

Pursuant to Civil Local Rule 16.1(c), within forty-five (45) days of the filing of an answer, or as otherwise ordered by the court, counsel and the parties shall appear before the magistrate judge supervising discovery for an early neutral evaluation conference. This appearance shall be made with authority to discuss and enter into settlement.

INITIAL SCHEDULING ORDER

An initial scheduling order will be issued by the magistrate judge assigned to the case. The scheduling order usually sets the following:

(1)   Date of discovery planning meeting pursuant to rule 26(f) of the Federal Rules of Civil Procedure;

(2)   Date to lodge discovery plan with the Court;

(3)   Date for initial disclosures under Rule 26(a)(1)(A)-(D); and

(4)   Date of the Case Management Conference.

CASE MANAGEMENT CONFERENCE

Counsel and parties will meet with the assigned magistrate judge for a Case Management Conference. Prior to the Case Management Conference counsel shall attempt to identify all discovery issues and endeavor to resolve any disputes. Procedures for the Case Management Conference are set forth in Local Rule 16.1(d).

Either during the case management conference, or shortly after, the magistrate judge will set, after consultation with the Court, the pre-trial and trial dates. Typically, the pre-trial date will be within three weeks of the trial date.

TEMPORARY RESTRAINING ORDERS/PRELIMINARY INJUNCTIONS

Temporary restraining orders and preliminary injunctions will be issued pursuant to Rule 65 of the Federal Rules of Civil Procedure. In extraordinary circumstances, temporary restraining orders may be heard ex parte, but otherwise the Court requires service on the other side before proceeding. Alternatively, the Court may issue a limited temporary restraining order to preserve the status quo pending further briefing on the issue. The Court will generally require the moving party to give notice of the date set for the hearing, if any, at least by telephone.

DISCOVERY & PROTECTIVE ORDERS

All motions to compel discovery are referred to the magistrate judge assigned to the case. The Magistrate Court will not entertain motions pursuant to Rules 26 through 37 of the Federal Rules of Civil Procedure unless counsel have previously met and conferred concerning all disputed issues. Civil Local Rule 26.1(a).

Protective orders shall issue only for good cause shown, pursuant to Rule 26(c) of the Federal Rules of Civil Procedure, and may be modified by the Court at anytime.

PRETRIAL CONFERENCE

Pursuant to Civil Local Rule 16.1(f)(7), the Court requires that the Plaintiff file the pretrial order no less than five days before the pretrial conference. The pretrial orders must include all elements set out in Civil Local Rule 16.1(f)(7)(c) and any other issues relevant to the trial. The Court expects all parties to cooperate in completing the pretrial order.

PRETRIAL MOTION PRACTICE

Pursuant to Civil Local Rule 7.1(b)(2), all dates for motion hearings may be obtained by calling the law clerk, but may be modified by Court Order. Briefing schedules are set forth in the Local Rules. There are no additional filing deadlines other than those set forth in the Local Rules, unless the Court sets a specific briefing schedule in the case. If the Court requires additional briefing, it will inform the parties.

Parties scheduling a motion beyond 28 calendar days need not be ready to file the motion within 48 hours of obtaining a hearing date from the law clerk. However, parties must still comply with the briefing schedules set forth in Civil Local Rule 7.1(e).

The Court may hear motions on the papers and without oral argument, in accordance with Civil Local Rule 7.1(d)(1). Unless informed otherwise, parties should assume that the Court will hear oral arguments in open court.

MOTIONS *IN LIMINE*

At the pretrial conference, the Court will set a date for motions *in limine*. If no separate briefing schedule is ordered by the Court, the parties should follow the 28-day motion filing schedule as set forth in the Local Rules to determine the filing deadline for the motions *in limine*, opposition, and reply.

TRIAL BRIEFS

Pursuant to the Local Rule 16.1(f)(9), the parties shall, no later than seven days prior to the date of trial: (1) serve and file all briefs on all significant disputed issues of law, including foreseeable procedural and evidentiary issues, setting forth briefly the party's positions and the supporting arguments and authorities; and (2) serve and file proposed *voir dire* questions and verdict forms.

Fourteen days before trial the parties shall file a "Joint Trial Brief" that sets forth:
(1)   Any facts the parties no longer dispute;
(2)   Copies of depositions to be offered into evidence;
(3)   Written waivers of claims or defenses, if any; and
(4)   An itemized statement of special damages, if applicable.

JURY SELECTION

The Court will consider a jury questionnaire when requested by a party not less than sixty (60) days before the trial date.

At the start of *voir dire*, the courtroom deputy will provide counsel with a list of the jury panel in the order they were randomly drawn in the jury lounge. The Court will conduct the initial jury *voir dire* and grant each side twenty (20) minutes of follow-up *voir dire*. The blind strike system regarding the exercise of peremptory challenges will be used. Generally, any challenges for cause/*Batson* issues will occur at sidebar.

VIDEO EQUIPMENT

If a party intends to use any special equipment, such as video projectors, slide projectors, tape recorders, or the like, they should notify the courtroom deputy seven days prior to the date of trial, and prepare and submit to the Court a draft Order listing all such equipment.

EXHIBITS

Each counsel should contact the courtroom deputy prior to numbering their exhibits. The courtroom deputy will assign a block of numbers to each counsel. No letters shall be used. Exhibit stickers may be obtained from the courtroom deputy clerk or the Intake Window of the Clerk's Office, in advance of the start of trial.

Exhibits are to be placed in three-ring binders separated by tabs. At the start of trial, unless ordered by the Court to do so earlier, the parties shall provide one copy of the exhibit notebooks to the Court.

Each counsel must keep counsel's own list of exhibits and should keep track when each has been admitted into evidence. The deputy clerk will have the official exhibit list. Once an exhibit is admitted it is the property of the court and must remain in the courtroom, unless otherwise ordered by the Court.

Counsel must show each other all exhibits, except for those intended to impeach witnesses. An exhibit must be admitted into evidence before counsel may show it to the jury. When referring to an exhibit, counsel should refer to its exhibit number whenever possible.

The Court, upon request, may permit truly significant exhibits to be passed to the jury. However, counsel should use this sparingly.

Pursuant to General order 340, at the conclusion of trial, all exhibits will be returned to the party who produced them.

TRIAL SCHEDULE

Trial generally proceeds from 9:00 a.m. to 4:30 p.m., Monday through Thursday, unless the Court schedules otherwise. Jury deliberations generally proceed from 9:00 a.m. to 4:30 p.m., unless the Court schedules otherwise. The Court will notify the parties of deviations from this schedule.

In civil trials, it is the practice of the Court to set a reasonable time limit for the entire trial. This time limit will reflect the estimates of counsel but is also based on the Court's independent assessment of the time necessary to complete the trial. The time limit set by the Court includes opening statements, arguments, testimony, and any other matters that occur over the course of the trial, excluding jury selection.

The Court will keep track of time limits and will inform the parties periodically of the time spent and remaining for trial, generally at the end of each trial day.

The time limit is subject to exception for good cause shown.

TRIAL PROCEDURE

The parties must provide opposing counsel with at least twenty-four (24) hours notice of the witnesses to be called to testify at trial on the succeeding day. The Court expects promptness from counsel and witnesses. It is counsel's duty to tell the Court on the first day of trial of any commitments in any other court on a subsequent day that may result in absence or late arrival. Due to the Court's schedule, counsel and witnesses are expected to be present for trial except for emergencies.

Lawyers must make every effort to have their witnesses available on the day they are to testify. The Court attempts to accommodate witnesses' schedules and may permit counsel to call them out of sequence if warranted by the circumstances. Counsel must anticipate any such possibility and discuss it with opposing counsel and the Court. Counsel must promptly alert the Court to any scheduling problems involving witnesses.

When counsel has the floor, the Court expects that opposing counsel will not distract the Court or jury by conversing audibly with their client or co-counsel, ostentatiously passing notes, rummaging through papers, or other conspicuous conduct.

OPENING STATEMENTS AND SUMMATION

Opening statements shall not include legal arguments and should not argue the case. Opening statements shall state only the facts that each party believes will be presented at trial.

The Court will pre-instruct the jury on the law prior to summation by counsel if requested to do so. Counsel are encouraged to use the law in their summations. After summation, the Court will give concluding instructions.

EXAMINATION OF WITNESSES

Counsel is responsible for furnishing the courtroom deputy with a current list of witnesses prior to commencement of trial. Except for young witnesses under age 14, counsel should address witnesses by their surnames, e.g., Mr. or Ms. A., Sergeant B, or Doctor C.

Counsel shall not assert their personal opinion as to the credibility of a witness, the culpability of a civil litigant, or the guilt or innocence of an accused. Nor shall counsel assert personal knowledge of a fact in issue, or assert a fact not in evidence. Counsel should not by facial expression, nodding or other conduct exhibit any opinion, adverse or favorable, concerning any testimony being given by a witness. Counsel should admonish counsel's own clients and witnesses to avoid such conduct.

Where a party has more than one counsel, only that counsel may conduct the direct or cross examination of a given witness and make any objections.

OBJECTIONS

When objecting, counsel must state the objection and state only that counsel objects and the legal ground of objection. If the Court needs additional information to rule on the objection, the Court will ask for further argument. Counsel should avoid arguing the objection in the presence of the jury and should not argue with the ruling of the Court in the presence of the jury. Such matters may be raised at the first recess without waiving any rights by such delayed motion.

MOTIONS DURING TRIAL

Counsel should not make oral motions (e.g., motions for mistrial) in the presence of the jury. Such motions may be made at the next recess without waiving any rights by the delay.

The Court will not hear motions that are brought for the first time in trial without a strong showing that counsel could not have filed them sooner. This includes admissibility questions. Most issues can be anticipated before trial. If any counsel raises during the trial a question of law that could not have been raised before trial, and may require research and/or briefing, counsel should give the Court advance notice when possible.

BENCH CONFERENCES

During a jury trial, the Court wishes to maximize the jury's time and therefore strongly discourages sidebar conferences while the jury is in the jury box. If counsel wishes to speak to the Court outside the jury's presence, counsel may request to do so at the start of a recess or at the end of the day. The Court will generally not grant requests to see the Court outside the presence of the jury when the Court is about to begin the day of trial or reconvene following a recess since these matters can generally await the next recess.

DEPOSITIONS

When possible, counsel should provide the Court with a list of deposition excerpts (page and line) that will be read in Court.

In using depositions of an adverse party for impeachment, either one of the following procedure may be adopted:

(1)   If counsel wishes to read the question and answer as alleged impeachment and ask the witness no further questions on the subject, counsel may read the relevant portions of the deposition into the record, stating the page and line where the reading began and the page and line where the reading ended; or

(2)   If counsel wishes to ask the witness further questions on the subject matter, the deposition is placed in front of the witness and the witness is told to read silently the pages and lines involved. Then counsel may either ask the witness further questions on the matter and there read the quotations or read the quotations and there ask the further questions.

Where a witness is absent and the witness's testimony is offered by deposition, please observe the following procedures:

(1)   In jury cases, a reader should occupy the witness chair and read the testimony of the witness while the examining counsel asks the questions, and if included, opposing counsel should read those questions posed by opposing counsel.

(2)   In non-jury cases, the above procedure is helpful if lengthy, but if brief, counsel may simply read from the entire deposition portion selected.

JURY INSTRUCTIONS

On the first day of trial, the parties should each submit proposed jury instructions to the Court <u>in hard copy and on disc</u>[1] on the first day of trial, unless otherwise ordered by the Court. Supplemental instructions should be filed and served as soon as the need becomes

---

[1]   WordPerfect 6.0 or higher.

apparent.

Jury instruction conferences are held after hours and are not part of the time allocated for the trial. Counsel must cite the authority supporting any proposed instructions. Any proposed modifications of instructions from statutory authority or the Ninth Circuit Models must state specifically the modification and the authority supporting the modification. All proposed instructions submitted by either party that the Court does not adopt will be deemed opposed.

Prior to the case being argued to the jury, the Court will generally provide each party with the jury instructions the Court intends to use. It is each party's responsibility to carefully review these jury instructions and make suggestions to the Court if modifications appear necessary.

JURY DELIBERATIONS

During jury deliberations, counsel for the parties must provide the courtroom deputy with a phone number where they may be reached. Counsel should remain within twenty (20) minutes of the Court during jury deliberations, but no party may remain in the courtroom or on that floor of the courthouse.

Counsel must not speak or interact with any jurors in the proceeding until after a verdict has been rendered. Counsel must instruct witnesses, clients, and observers not to have any interaction with the jurors.

Hon. Larry Alan Burns
District Judge

Chambers Information
U.S. District Court, Southern District of California
Courtroom 9, 2nd Floor
940 Front Street
San Diego, CA 92101

Scheduling Information
Courtroom Deputy: (619) 557-6038

Criminal Matters	Mondays at 9:30 a.m. and 2:00 p.m.

Biographical Information
Born 1954 in Pasadena, CA

Federal Judicial Service:
- Judge, U. S. District Court, Southern District of California
- Nominated by George W. Bush on May 1, 2003, to a new seat created by 116 Stat. 1758;
Confirmed by the Senate on September 24, 2003, and received commission on September 25, 2003.
- U.S. Magistrate Judge, U.S. District Court for the Southern District of California, 1997-2003

Education:
- Point Loma College, B.A., 1976
- University of San Diego School of Law, J.D., 1979

Professional Career:
- Deputy District Attorney, San Diego County, California, 1979-1985
- Assistant U.S. Attorney, Southern District of California, 1985-1997

I.   **Judge Burns' Case Management Orders**
A.   *Standing Order in Civil Cases*

STANDING ORDER IN CIVIL CASES

1.   **LOCAL RULES**

Except as otherwise provided in this Standing Order or as ordered by the Court, all parties are expected to strictly adhere to the Local Rules of this District.

2.   **DISCOVERY**

Pursuant to Civil Local Rules 26.1(e) and 72.1(b), discovery matters are generally handled by the assigned Magistrate Judge. The words "**DISCOVERY MATTER**" shall appear in the caption of all documents relating to discovery to ensure proper routing. Counsel shall contact the law clerk of the assigned Magistrate Judge to schedule hearings on discovery matters.

3.   **SETTLEMENT**

a.   Any stipulation for dismissal presuming the Court will retain jurisdiction will be rejected unless: (1) it is accompanied by a Consent to Exercise of Jurisdiction by a United States Magistrate Judge over all disputes arising out of the settlement agreement, including interpretation and enforcement of the terms of the settlement agreement, *signed by all parties and their counsel*; and (2) it includes in the stipulation text and in the proposed order the following language:

> The Magistrate Judge shall retain jurisdiction over all disputes between and among the parties arising out of the settlement agreement, including but not limited to interpretation and enforcement of the terms of the settlement agreement.

b.   Class Actions: Any proposed order for preliminary approval of class certification or preliminary settlement approval will be rejected unless accompanied by an affidavit and memorandum of points and authorities establishing all requirements have been satisfied, including the class certification factors and fairness factors. If the proposed order also seeks approval of class notice, the affidavit and memorandum of points and authorities shall also address compliance with all applicable procedural rules and statutory provisions.

4.   **MOTIONS**

a.   Time of Filing and Service of Moving Papers: Regardless of the motion hearing date, the moving party shall file all moving papers within three court days of obtaining the hearing date from chambers, or within the time provided by Civil Local Rule 7.1(e)(1), whichever is earlier. The moving papers shall be served at the time of filing.

b.   Points and Authorities: In their memoranda of points and authorities, the parties shall state all legal and factual bases for their respective positions. An opposing party's failure to file a memorandum of points and authorities in opposition to any motion will be construed as consent to granting the motion.

c.   <u>Lodgments of Exhibits:</u> The party lodging exhibits pursuant to Civil Local Rule 1.1(e)(15), shall provide an original and one copy for the Court's use as provided in Civil Local Rule 5.1(i)(1).

d.   <u>Audio or Video Exhibits:</u> Any party desiring to rely on audio or video materials as exhibits to his or her motion papers, shall contemporaneously file a transcript of the audio or video materials. The transcript shall either be certified by a court reporter or stipulated to by the opposing party. Any audio or video materials not complying with these requirements will be rejected.

e.   <u>Summary Judgment/Adjudication:</u> In any pending motion for summary judgment or summary adjudication, no later than ten court days prior to the date of the hearing, the parties are ordered to meet, confer and submit a Joint Statement of Undisputed Facts. Only one joint statement of undisputed facts, signed by all parties, shall be filed. Statements of undisputed facts not jointly submitted will be rejected. Any objections to evidence filed in support of the moving party's reply shall be served and filed no later than three court days prior to the date initially set for hearing.

f.   <u>Oral Argument:</u> The Court may hear oral argument on motions in appropriate cases <u>when specifically requested by a party</u>. When oral argument is granted, the Court will notify the parties at least three days before the scheduled hearing. In cases in which oral argument is not granted by the Court, the matter will be considered submitted for decision on the papers pursuant to Civil Local Rule 7.1(d).

g.   Argument by Telephonic Conference: Any requests for argument by telephonic conference pursuant to Civil Local Rule 7.1(d)(3) shall be made no later than three court days before the scheduled hearing.

h.   <u>Americans With Disability Act Cases:</u> No hearing dates for Motions For Summary Judgment or for Preliminary Injunctions will be given in ADA cases until after the Early Neutral Evaluation Conference has occurred.

i.   <u>*Amicus Curiae* Briefs:</u> The court discourages requests to file *amici curiae* briefs for the reasons discussed in *Voices For Choices v. Illinois Bell Telephone Co.*, 339 F.3d 542 (7th Cir. 2003). Counsel must obtain leave before submitting such a brief for the court's consideration.

j.   <u>Applications for Reconsideration:</u> **Motions for reconsideration are disfavored unless a party shows there is new evidence, a change in controlling law, or establishes that the Court committed clear error in the earlier ruling.** No motion for reconsideration will be filed without leave of Court. No later than the time provided in Civil Local Rule 7.1(i)(2), the party desiring to move for reconsideration shall file an *ex parte* application for leave to file a motion to reconsider. The *ex parte* application shall be accompanied by a declaration as required by Civil Local Rule 7.1(i)(1). The *ex parte* application shall contain a brief summary of the argument the party intends to present in a motion for reconsideration, and shall not exceed five pages in length. Upon review of the *ex parte* application, the Court will either issue an order granting leave to file a motion for reconsideration, including a briefing schedule, or an order denying leave.

5.   **TEMPORARY RESTRAINING ORDERS/MOTIONS FOR EMERGENCY RELIEF**

All motions for temporary restraining orders or other emergency relief shall be briefed. While temporary restraining orders may be heard *ex parte*, the Court will do so only in extraordinary circumstances. The Court's strong preference is for the opposing party to be served, and afforded a reasonable opportunity to file an opposition. In appropriate cases, the Court may issue a limited restraining order to preserve evidence pending further briefing on the issue. The Court will generally give notice of hearing by telephone.

6.   ***MARKMAN* HEARINGS AND TUTORIAL SESSIONS**

a.   *Hearing Dates:* All hearing dates for *Markman* hearings and tutorial sessions shall be obtained from the clerk of the judge to whom the case is assigned. Typically, the tutorial session and *Markman* hearing will be held on the same date, with the tutorial session immediately preceding the *Markman* hearing.

b.   Meeting and Conference: Prior to filing any papers for the tutorial session and *Markman* hearing, parties shall meet and confer for purposes of arriving at an agreed construction for as many claims as possible, assembling a Joint Appendix of Exhibits, and, if possible, preparing of a joint tutorial session.

c.   Time of Filing: No later than two weeks before the hearing date, parties shall file a Joint Claim Construction Chart, Joint Appendix of Exhibits, and, if necessary, claim construction briefs. Courtesy copies of all papers filed for the tutorial session and *Markman* hearing shall be submitted to chambers no later than two weeks before the hearing date.

d.   Joint Appendix of Exhibits: To avoid unnecessary duplication of exhibits, parties shall file a Joint Appendix of Exhibits. Where five or more exhibits are filed, or where exhibits exceed five hundred pages, the courtesy copy of exhibits shall be submitted in three-ring binders with side tabs, accompanied by an index.

e.   Joint Claim Construction Chart: The Joint Claim Construction Chart shall be prepared on legal-sized paper in landscape format. The chart shall consist of five columns: (1) the verbatim claim language; (2) the agreed construction, if any; (3) the plaintiff's proposed construction; (4) the defendant's proposed construction; and (5) a blank column for the Court's use. The chart shall number the claims (1, 2, 3, etc.) and label each claim limitation with a letter (a, b, c, etc). (For a good example, parties may refer to the Joint Claim Construction Chart filed in *QUALCOMM, Inc. v. Conexant Sys., Inc. et al.*, case no. 02cv2002 B (JFS), filed Sept. 27, 2004.)

f.   Tutorial Session: Parties will have an opportunity to present a tutorial session on the record to educate the Court. They shall address solely the technology of the patent subject matter (i.e., not the product). The tutorial session is not a forum for legal argument, and, where possible, the parties should jointly present the tutorial.

g.   <u>Electronic, Video or Audio Equipment:</u> Parties shall notify the courtroom deputy **at least five court days in advance of** the tutorial session or *Markman* hearing of any electronic, video or audio equipment they intend to use, and shall prepare and submit to the Court a draft order authorizing the use in the courtroom of all such equipment.

7.   REQUESTS TO SEAL DOCUMENTS

Before submitting any document for filing under seal as provided by Civil Local Rule 79.2(c), a party must make an *ex parte* application for leave to file documents under seal. The application must address pertinent legal authorities.

8.   *EX PARTE* APPLICATIONS AND MISCELLANEOUS ADMINISTRATIVE REQUESTS

Before filing any *ex parte* application, counsel shall meet and confer in an attempt to informally resolve the issue. All miscellaneous administrative requests and *ex parte* applications are considered on the papers and may not be set for a hearing. Any *ex parte* application must be supported by a declaration, must certify the parties have met and conferred, and must make the required showing according to the applicable legal standard. Unless expressly provided otherwise herein, or in the Local Rules, this Court will consider *ex parte* applications only when a basis for extraordinary relief is shown. Sanctions may be imposed for misuse of *ex parte* applications. Any *ex parte* application filed with the Court shall be served on the opposing counsel via facsimile or overnight mail. *Ex parte* applications not opposed within two court days will be considered unopposed and may be granted on that ground.

9.   OBJECTIONS TO MAGISTRATE JUDGES' DECISIONS

a.   <u>Non-Dispositive Matters Pursuant to 28 U.S.C. § 636(b)(1)(A):</u> A party objecting to a Magistrate Judge's order shall file objections as provided in Federal Rule of Civil Procedure 72. Upon receipt of objections, the Court will issue a briefing schedule and set a hearing date, if appropriate.

b.   <u>Reports and Recommendations Pursuant to 28 U.S.C. § 636(b)(1)(B):</u> A party objecting to a Magistrate Judge's Report and Recommendation shall file objections, if any, within the time provided in the Report and Recommendation. Any response or reply brief must be filed within the time specified therein. If no briefing schedule is specified in the Report and Recommendation, the objecting party shall follow the time limits provided in section 636(b). The Court will set a briefing schedule upon receipt of timely objections.

10.   CONTINUANCES

Parties requesting a continuance of any conference, hearing, deadline, briefing schedule, or other procedural changes, shall meet and confer prior to making any requests to the Court. If an agreement is reached, the parties shall submit a stipulation and proposed order (*see* Civil Local Rule 7.2). If no agreement is reached, the requesting party shall file an *ex parte* application as provided herein. Any request for a continuance, whether stipulated or not, shall state: (1) the original date; (2) the number of previous requests for continuance; (3) whether previous requests were granted or denied; (4) a showing of good cause particularly focusing upon evidence of diligence by the party seeking delay and of prejudice that may result if a continuance is denied; (5) if applicable, the reasons stated by the opposing party for refusing to consent; and (6) whether the requested continuance affects other case management dates.

Except in extraordinary circumstances, stipulations to amend a briefing schedule or to continue a motion hearing date must be filed no later than three court days before the affected date.

Unless otherwise ordered by the Court, the rescheduling of a motion hearing date does not change the date on which an opposition brief or reply brief is due; any opposition and reply briefs remain due on the dates provided in Civil Local Rule 7.1(e), calculated based on the date initially set for hearing.

11.   *PRO SE* PRISONER CASES

In cases involving *pro se* prisoners as litigants, the Court expects defense counsel and the government entity with which a defendant is associated to cooperate in facilitating the prisoner's telephonic appearances or personal appearances for any scheduled conference, hearing or trial. This responsibility includes preparing any writs of *habeas corpus ad testificandum* for the incarcerated *pro se* plaintiff and any of his or her incarcerated witnesses, as authorized by the Court.

12.   PRETRIAL CONFERENCES AND PREPARATION FOR TRIAL

a.   Memorandum of Contentions of Fact and Law: The requirement to file Memoranda of Contentions of Fact and Law pursuant to Civil Local Rule 16.1(f) is waived. The parties shall instead focus their efforts on timely drafting and submitting a proposed pretrial order as provided by Civil Local Rule 16.1(f).

b.   Proposed Pretrial Order: Civil Local Rule 16.1(f) provides detailed instructions for the preparation of a proposed pretrial order. The Court expects parties to strictly adhere to these instructions, and to include in the proposed pretrial order all required information and any other issues relevant to the trial. In addition, in jury trial cases, the parties are encouraged to stipulate to a non-unanimous verdict. To this end, the parties shall include in their proposed pretrial order a statement indicating whether they will stipulate to the following:

(a)   The Court will impanel eight jurors – six regular jurors and two alternates;

(b)   At the end of the trial, all remaining jurors will be entitled to vote;

(c)   The verdict need not be unanimous, but may be decided as follows:

> 8 of 10
> 7 of 9
> 6 of 8
> 5 of 7
> 4 of 6

Failure to comply or cooperate in complying with the Civil Local Rules and this directive regarding the proposed pretrial order may result in sanctions.

c.   Pretrial Conference: In addition to the issues listed in Civil Local Rule 16.1(f), counsel should arrive prepared to discuss the following: (1) scheduling; (2) order of proof and reasonable time limits; (3) questions relating to proof, such as stipulations of fact, stipulations to the authenticity of documents, foundation and admissibility of documentary evidence and depositions, advance rulings on admissibility of evidence, if appropriate, and any anticipated motions *in limine*; (4) bifurcation or separate trial if necessary or appropriate; (5) any need for special procedures to deal with complex issues or multiple parties; (6) need for interpreters or any other special needs; (7) issues of foreign law that reasonably would be expected to be a part of the proceedings (notice of such issues and contentions about the applicability of foreign law must be provided no later than the pretrial conference and should be incorporated in the proposed pretrial order to give the parties ample opportunity to marshal resources and evidence or experts pertinent to the foreign law issues); and (8) elimination of frivolous claims and defenses before trial.

d.   Trial Date and Time Limits: A trial date will typically be set at the pretrial conference. In consultation with counsel at the pretrial conference, the Court will generally set reasonable time limits for the trial. The time limits will reflect the estimates of counsel, but will also be based on the Court's independent assessment of the time necessary to complete the trial. When set by the Court, time limits are all-inclusive, including the jury instructions conference, jury selection, opening statements, argument, and any other matters that occur over the course of the trial. Time limits are subject to modification for good cause shown.

e.   Motions *in Limine*: Before filing any motion *in limine*, parties shall meet and confer and attempt to resolve their disputes. The Court will typically set a briefing schedule and hearing date for motions *in limine* at the pretrial conference. If no separate briefing schedule is ordered by the Court, any motion *in limine* shall be filed and served no later than six weeks before the date initially set for trial, and shall include the counsel's affidavit certifying the parties have met and conferred. Any opposition shall be filed and served no later than five weeks before the date initially set for trial. Any reply shall be filed and served no later than four weeks before the date initially set for trial. Parties should not present summary judgment motions or motions to dismiss under the label of motions *in limine* as the Court will not rule on any such motions presented in that fashion.

f.   Trial Briefs: In bench trial cases, trial briefs shall be served and filed no later than 14 calendar days before the date initially set for trial. In addition to the provisions in Civil Local Rule 16.1(f), the trial briefs shall analyze the legal basis for each cause of action, request for relief and defense to be tried.

g.   Final Witness and Exhibit Lists: **No later than five court days before trial**, the parties shall exchange and submit to chambers their final witness and exhibit lists. Each party shall submit one extra copy of the witness list (for the court reporter), and two extra copies of the exhibit list (for the court reporter and the courtroom deputy). Unless otherwise ordered by the Court, the final witness and exhibit lists shall not contain any witnesses or exhibits which were not included in the pretrial order. For bench trials, the parties shall also deliver to chambers the bench copy of their exhibits no later than five court days before trial.

h.   Joint Statement of the Case: **No later than five court days before trial**, the parties shall submit to chambers a joint brief description of the case to be read to the jury.

i.   Proposed Jury Instructions:

(a)   The parties are required to **jointly** file one set of agreed-upon instructions **no later than ten court days before the date initially set for trial**. To this end, parties shall exchange their proposed jury instructions **at least three weeks before the date initially set for trial**. The parties shall then meet and confer to prepare the agreed-upon set of instructions.

(b)   If the parties cannot agree upon one complete set of instructions, they shall jointly file one set of those instructions they have agreed upon, and each party shall file and serve **no later than ten court days before the date initially set for trial** a supplemental set of instructions not agreed upon, together with all objections raised to the opposing party's proposed instruction on the same issue. Any objection shall set forth the objected-to instruction in its entirety, identify the objected-to portion(s), provide legal authority explaining why the instruction is improper, and include a concise statement of argument concerning the instruction. Where applicable, the objecting party shall submit an alternative instruction covering the subject or legal principle at issue.

(c)   Additional jury instructions may be filed and served as soon as the need for them becomes apparent.

(d)   The Court prefers to use form instructions, such as the Ninth Circuit model instructions, BAJI or CACI where applicable. Any proposed modifications from the statutory law or form instructions must clearly delineate each modification and state the reason or authority for it.

(e)   The parties shall submit directly to chambers two copies of any jury instructions in the following format:

(i)   **Faxed copies of jury instructions will be rejected.**

(ii)   All proposed instructions shall be double-spaced and printed in 14 point Times New Roman font.

(iii)   The first copy shall state the instruction, its source, and the authority supporting the instruction.

(iv)   The second copy shall contain only the proposed instruction with no other marks or writing except for the heading "COURT'S INSTRUCTION NO. ___" with the number left blank. It shall be typed in 14 point Times New Roman font, double-spaced, and printed on plain, unlined, unnumbered paper.

(v)   All instructions should be short, concise and neutral statements of the law. Argumentative instructions will not be given and should not be submitted.

(vi)   All counsel will be provided with a copy of the final instructions before the Court reads them to the jury.

j.   <u>Electronic, Video or Audio Equipment:</u> Parties shall notify the courtroom deputy **at least five court days before trial** of any electronic, video or audio equipment they intend to use during trial, and prepare and submit to the Court a draft order authorizing the use in the courtroom of all such equipment.

k.   <u>Jury Selection:</u> Unless authorized by the Court, parties should not submit jury questionnaires. The courtroom deputy will provide counsel with a list of the jury panel in random order before *voir dire*.

The courtroom deputy will seat all prospective jurors (20 prospective jurors will generally be summoned for civil cases). The Court will conduct the initial jury *voir dire*. In appropriate cases, the Court may permit follow-up *voir dire* by the attorneys.

After *voir dire* of the entire panel has been completed, counsel may make any challenges for cause at side bar. If a challenge for cause is sustained, the excluded panelist will remain in his or her seat for the time being.

Counsel will next exercise peremptory challenges using the "Double Blind Method," whereby the parties simultaneously exercise their challenges.

After each side has exercised its peremptory challenges, the first eight persons not challenged peremptorily or successfully challenged for cause shall constitute the jury. All remaining prospective jurors will be excused at that time.

13.   TRIALS

The Court expects counsel and witnesses to be on time.

a.   <u>Witnesses:</u> All counsel shall make every effort to have their witnesses available all day on the day the witnesses are to testify. The Court will attempt to accommodate witnesses' schedules and will generally permit witnesses to testify out of sequence, if necessary. Counsel shall anticipate the need for witnesses to be available and, if there is any question, discuss it with opposing counsel or with the Court. Counsel shall promptly alert the Court to any scheduling problems involving witnesses.

b.   Exhibits: **Before the court session in which an exhibit is to be referred to or offered in evidence, the exhibit shall be pre-marked for identification in the lower right corner using labels available from the Clerk's Office.** Exhibits must be admitted in evidence before they are displayed to the jury.

Any party seeking monetary damages shall prepare a summary of the documentary evidence supporting the claim for monetary damages (e.g., medical bills, accounts, etc.).

c.   Deposition Transcripts: The following guidelines shall apply to deposition testimony offered in evidence: Before trial commences, the parties shall meet and confer, agree on and designate all deposition testimony intended to be read into evidence. The proponent of deposition testimony shall prepare a clean copy of the excerpted testimony, indicating the beginning and ending page and line numbers. This shall be given to the Court and placed in the record. The court reporter will not be required to transcribe the deposition testimony as it is read.

d.   Audio and Video Presentations: The procedures set forth above for admitting deposition transcripts shall apply. The proponent of any audio or video testimonial evidence shall prepare a written transcript of the evidence. Before trial commences, the parties shall meet, confer, and agree on a stipulated transcript. If the parties cannot agree, each side shall prepare and submit to the Court prior to trial its own version of the disputed portion of the audio or video testimonial evidence.

e.   Bench Conferences: Sidebar conferences are discouraged. Requests to speak to the Court outside the jury's presence should be made at the start of a recess or at the end of the trial day. The Court will not grant requests for conferences out of the jury's presence at the beginning of the trial day or following a recess.

f.   Jury Fees: The expense of empaneling a jury for a trial shall be taxed equally to the parties if the case settles after a jury has been summoned.

14.   COMMUNICATION WITH THE COURT OR CHAMBERS

Consistent with Civil Local Rule 83.9, attorneys and parties shall refrain from writing letters or placing telephone calls to the Court or sending the Court copies of letters addressed to others, or otherwise causing unauthorized ex parte communications with the Court. Instead, all matters for the Court's attention shall be formally submitted in compliance with the Local Rules, the Federal Rules of Civil Procedure, and the Federal Rules of Evidence.

Absent unavoidable circumstances, counsel shall **personally** initiate any authorized communications with the Court or with chambers staff, rather than rely on a representative (e.g., a secretary or paralegal).

Any authorized telephonic communications with the Court or chambers staff regarding disputed issues must be initiated with all concerned counsel on the line.

15.   NOTICE OF THIS ORDER

Counsel for plaintiff, or plaintiff, if appearing on his or her own behalf, is responsible for promptly serving notice of these requirements upon defendant's counsel, or defendant, if appearing on his or her own behalf. If the action came to the Court via a noticed removal, this burden falls to the removing defendant.

B. *Standing Order in Criminal Cases*

STANDING ORDER IN CRIMINAL CASES

1.   CALENDAR

Criminal matters are heard on Mondays at 9:30 AM and 2:00 PM, unless otherwise scheduled by the Court. Except for emergency hearings, counsel must contact the courtroom deputy by **12:30 PM** the Friday before the requested hearing date to have a matter placed on calendar.

2.   MOTIONS

All motions, except motions *in limine* and those pertaining to sentencing matters, shall be filed at least **21 calendar days** before the hearing date. Opposition briefs shall be filed at least **7 calendar days** before the hearing date.

Motions *in limine* shall be filed **7 calendar days** before the hearing date.

Applications for Orders Shortening Time are disfavored, and must be supported by a non-conclusory affidavit signed by counsel setting forth facts establishing specific good cause. *An original and two copies of the Application shall be submitted directly to chambers,* **not filed with the Clerk's Office.**

In the event of a disposition in any case calendared for motion hearing, **both** counsel shall notify the courtroom deputy at the earliest possible time of the fact of the disposition and request that the motion hearing date be vacated.

Motions pertaining to Guidelines sentencing and other sentencing recommendations shall be filed at least **13 calendar days** before the sentencing hearing date. Responses or oppositions to motions pertaining to sentencing recommendations and all other sentencing memoranda shall be filed at least **5 calendar days** before the sentencing hearing date. **All counsel shall strictly adhere to Crim. L.R. 32.1(a)(9), which provides that sentencing summary charts setting forth pertinent Guidelines calculations shall be** submitted directly to chambers **at least 5 calendar days before the sentencing hearing.**

A party requesting a continuance of a sentencing hearing must notify the courtroom deputy at the earliest possible time, **but in no event later than the Friday before the scheduled sentencing date.**

3.   EVIDENTIARY SUBMISSIONS MUST CONFORM WITH
LOCAL RULES

All motions and oppositions to motions shall, **at the time of initial filing**, comply with Crim. L.R. 47.1(g)(1) and (2), which provide that criminal motions requiring a predicate factual finding (e.g., motions to suppress statements on *Miranda* or voluntariness grounds) shall be supported by declarations, filed under penalty of perjury, and shall set forth all facts then known and upon which it is contended the motion should be granted or denied.

4.   PRETRIAL RELEASE

Pretrial release decisions and modifications of release conditions are to be made by the Magistrate Judge, subject to appeal. The Court will hear appeals on an emergency basis, provided that counsel appealing a pretrial release decision has served notice on the opposing party at least **24 hours before the hearing** and has supplied the Court with a transcript of the hearing before the Magistrate Judge.

5. RULE 11 GUILTY PLEAS

Unless the parties anticipate immediate sentencing, the Court encourages **all** Rule 11 guilty pleas to be entered before a Magistrate Judge.

6. TRIAL BRIEFS AND PROPOSED *VOIR DIRE* QUESTIONS

Parties may file trial briefs with the Court no later than **5 calendar days** before trial is to begin. A party should file a trial brief with the Court if there is any significant disputed issue of law, or if a party is requesting that specific questions be asked or specific topics be covered during the Court's *voir dire*.

7. TRIAL PROCEDURE

The Court expects counsel and witnesses to be on time.

All counsel shall make every effort to have their witnesses available all day on the day the witnesses are to testify. The Court will attempt to accommodate witnesses' schedules and will generally permit witnesses to testify out of sequence, if necessary. Counsel shall anticipate the need for witnesses to be available and, if there is any question, discuss it with opposing counsel or with the Court. Counsel shall promptly alert the Court to any scheduling problems involving witnesses.

Defense counsel shall arrange before trial for in-custody clients to be dressed out.

8. EXHIBITS

All exhibits offered by a party must be pre-marked for identification before the court session in which the exhibit is to be referred to or offered in evidence.

Government counsel shall provide the courtroom deputy with a list of exhibits before trial begins.

Exhibits must be admitted in evidence before they are displayed to the jury.

9. BENCH CONFERENCES

Sidebar conferences are discouraged and rarely granted. Requests to speak to the Court outside the jury's presence should be made at the start of a recess or at the end of the trial day.

The Court will not grant requests for conferences out of the jury's presence at the beginning of the trial day or following a recess.

10. JURY INSTRUCTIONS

The Court uses Ninth Circuit Model Criminal Jury Instructions, and gives standard instructions in every criminal case. Counsel for the government shall submit proposed Model Instructions defining the elements of the offense(s) to be tried. All counsel will be provided with a written copy of the final instructions before the Court reads them to the jury.

A party may propose appropriate modifications to the Model Instructions. Proposed modifications to the Model Instructions must clearly delineate the modification and the reason or authority for it. All other non-standard proposed instructions (e.g., theory of defense) shall be submitted in duplicate and adhere to the following format:

> a. The first copy shall contain the instruction and the authority supporting the instruction;
>
> b. The second copy shall contain only the proposed instruction with no

other marks or writing except for the heading "COURT'S INSTRUCTION NO. ___" with the number left blank. It shall be double-spaced and printed on unlined, unnumbered paper, in 14 point Times New Roman font.

Proposed jury instructions from all parties must be filed with the Court and served on all parties no later than the Friday before trial is to begin. Supplemental instructions must be filed with the Court and served on all parties as soon as the need for them becomes apparent.

11. COMMUNICATION WITH THE COURT OR CHAMBERS

Absent unavoidable circumstances, counsel shall personally initiate any authorized communication with the Court or with chambers staff, rather than rely on a representative (e.g., law clerk, secretary or paralegal).

Consistent with Civ. L.R. 83.9 (incorporated to criminal actions by Crim. L.R. 1.1(e)), attorneys and parties shall refrain from writing letters to the Court or sending the Court copies of letters addressed to others, or otherwise causing unauthorized *ex parte* correspondence to be delivered to chambers. Instead, all matters for the Court's attention shall be formally submitted in compliance with the Local Rules, the Federal Rules of Criminal Procedure, and the Federal Rules of Evidence.

Hon. Irma E. Gonzalez
District Judge

Chambers Information
U.S. District Court, Southern District of California
Courtroom 1, 4th Floor
940 Front Street
San Diego, CA 92101

Scheduling Information
Courtroom Deputy: (619) 557-6421

Biographical Information
Born 1948 in Palo Alto, CA

Federal Judicial Service:
- Judge, U. S. District Court, Southern District of California
- Nominated by George H.W. Bush on April 9, 1992, to a seat vacated by J. Lawrence Irving; Confirmed by the Senate on August 11, 1992, and received commission on August 12, 1992. Served as chief judge, 2005-2012.
- U.S. Magistrate, U.S. District Court for the Southern District of California, 1984-1991

Education:
- Stanford University, B.A., 1970
- University of Arizona College of Law, J.D., 1973

Professional Career:
- Law clerk, Hon. William C. Frey, U.S. District Court, District of Arizona, 1973-1975
- Assistant U.S. attorney, Criminal Division, U.S. Attorney's Office, Arizona, 1975-1979
- Trial attorney, U.S. Department of Justice, Antitrust Division, Los Angeles, California, 1979
- Assistant U.S. attorney, Criminal Division, U.S. Attorney's Office, Central District of California, 1979-1981
- Private practice, San Diego, California, 1981-1984
- Judge, California Superior Court, San Diego County, 1991-1992

Hon. William Q. Hayes
District Judge

Chambers Information
U.S. District Court, Southern District of California
Courtroom 4, 4th Floor
940 Front Street
San Diego, CA 92101

Scheduling Information
Courtroom Deputy: (619) 557-7360

Criminal Matters	Mondays at 9:00 a.m. and 2:00 p.m.

Biographical Information
Born 1956 in Bronxville, NY

Federal Judicial Service:
- Judge, U. S. District Court, Southern District of California
- Nominated by George W. Bush on May 1, 2003, to a new seat created by 116 Stat. 1758;
Confirmed by the Senate on October 2, 2003, and received commission on October 6, 2003.

Education:
- Syracuse University, B.S., 1978
- Syracuse University School of Law, J.D., 1983
- Syracuse University Graduate School of Business, M.B.A., 1983

Professional Career:
- Private Practice, 1983-1986
- Adjunct Faculty, National College, 1984-1985
- Adjunct Faculty, University of Colorado at Denver, 1985-1986
- Chief, Criminal Division, U.S. Attorney's Office, Southern District of California, 1987-2003
- Adjunct Faculty, Thomas Jefferson School of Law, 1989-1996
- Adjunct Faculty, University of San Diego Law School, 1998

I.   **Judge Hayes' Procedures and Practices**
      A.   *Civil Pretrial and Trial Procedures*

CIVIL PRETRIAL AND TRIAL PROCEDURES

The Court may vary these procedures as appropriate in any case. Counsel and pro se litigants must strictly adhere to all Court Orders. Unless otherwise ordered by the Court, counsel and pro se litigants are expected to follow the Federal Rules of Civil Procedure, the Local Rules for the Southern District of California, the Electronic Case Filing Administrative Policies and Procedures Manual, and any other applicable rules. The Local Rules and the Electronic Case Filing Administrative Policies and Procedures Manual are available on the Court's website: www.casd.uscourts.gov.

COMMUNICATION WITH CHAMBERS

Telephone calls to chambers are permitted only for scheduling or calendaring motion hearings or as otherwise authorized by the Court. Court personnel are prohibited from interpreting orders, discussing the merits of a case, or giving legal advice, including advice on procedural matters. Court personnel are prohibited from engaging in conference calls. Letters, faxes, and emails are prohibited unless otherwise authorized by the Court.

DISCOVERY

Counsel shall contact the magistrate judge's chambers directly for all matters pertaining to discovery. Any objection to a discovery ruling of the magistrate judge must be filed as a motion pursuant to Civil Local Rule 7.1.

PROPOSED ORDERS

Proposed orders shall be submitted in Word or WordPerfect format simultaneously with all motions, except motions that are fully noticed and set for hearing at least 28 days beyond the date of filing. In accordance with Section 2(h) of the Electronic Case Filing Administrative Policies and Procedures Manual, proposed orders shall not contain the name and law firm information of the filing party, and shall not contain the word "proposed" in the caption. Counsel shall email proposed orders to opposing counsel and to the following address: efile_hayes@casd.uscourts.gov, and include the docket number and case name in the subject line of the email.

JOINT MOTIONS/STIPULATIONS

Pursuant to Section 2(f)(4) of the Electronic Case Filing Administrative Policies and Procedures Manual, all stipulations must be filed as joint motions. Joint motions must be signed by the Court to have legal effect.

EX PARTE MOTIONS

The Court may rule upon ex parte motions without requiring a response from the opposing party. If a party intends to oppose the ex parte motion, the party must immediately file a notice stating that the party intends to oppose the ex parte motion and providing the date upon which the opposition will be filed.

PRETRIAL MOTION PRACTICE

Pursuant to Civil Local Rule 7.1(b), all dates for motion hearings must be obtained by calling the law clerk, but may be modified by the Court. After obtaining a hearing date from the law clerk, the party must file its motion within three (3) court days. A party who fails to file its papers within three (3) court days of obtaining the hearing date forfeits the assigned hearing date.

The Court may resolve motions on the papers and without oral argument, in accordance with Civil Local Rule 7.1(d)(1). Unless otherwise notified by the Court, the parties shall include the following language on the front of their motions directly underneath the hearing date: **"NO ORAL ARGUMENT UNLESS REQUESTED BY THE COURT."** This serves as notice to the parties that there will be no personal appearances at the hearing. If the Court decides to hear oral argument, the Court will contact the parties to schedule a time and/or issue an order setting the matter for oral argument.

An opposing party's failure to file an opposition to any motion may be construed as consent to the granting of the motion pursuant to Civil Local Rule 7.1(f)(3)(c).

All motions for summary judgment shall be accompanied by a separate statement of undisputed material facts. Any opposition to a summary judgment motion shall include a response to the separate statement of undisputed material facts.

COURTESY COPIES

Courtesy copies of filings that exceed 20 pages in length, including attachments and exhibits, shall be submitted in accordance with Section 2(e) of the Electronic Case Filing Administrative Policies and Procedures via United States Postal Service mail, courier, or delivery to chambers. The courtesy copy shall contain the CM/ECF document header on the top of each page. The Court prefers courtesy copies to be printed double-sided, but will accept single-sided. If a filing has more than three (3) exhibits, the exhibits must be tabbed.

TENTATIVE RULINGS

Judge Hayes does not issue tentative rulings.

ELECTRONIC, AUDIO/VIDEO, AND OTHER EQUIPMENT

The parties shall file a joint motion, or an ex parte motion if joint motion is not possible, requesting permission to use any electronic, audio/video, or other equipment in the courtroom at least seven (7) days before the hearing or trial and email a proposed order to the Court. The proposed order shall itemize all equipment and list the dates when it will be used in the courtroom. The order must be presented to security personnel when the equipment is brought into the courthouse.

TELEPHONIC HEARINGS

Unless otherwise ordered by the Court, all oral argument must be attended by counsel in person, and will be heard in open court. If a telephonic hearing is allowed by the Court, counsel appearing telephonically are responsible for arranging the call and shall email the Court the correct phone number and any dial-in information at least seven (7) days in advance of the hearing. Counsel shall be available at least five (5) minutes prior to the scheduled hearing time.

PRETRIAL CONFERENCE

Pursuant to Civil Local Rule 16.1(f)(6), the Court requires that the parties file and email to Chambers a proposed pretrial order at least seven (7) days before the pretrial conference. The proposed pretrial order must include all elements set out in Civil Local Rule 16.1(f)(6)(c) and any other issues relevant to the trial. All parties are required to cooperate in completing the proposed pretrial order.

The Court will set a trial date during the pretrial conference. The Court will also schedule a motion in limine hearing date during the pretrial conference. All motions in limine are due two weeks before the motion in limine hearing date. All responses are due seven (7) days before the motion in limine hearing date. Unless otherwise ordered by the Court, the joint proposed jury instructions, proposed verdict form, voir dire questions, statement of the case, exhibit binders and proposed verdict forms are also due seven (7) days before the motion in limine hearing date. The proposed jury instructions, proposed verdict form, and statement of the case shall also be emailed to the Court in Word or WordPerfect format.

EXHIBITS

Exhibit stickers may be obtained from the Clerk of the Court, in advance of the start of trial.

Exhibits are to be placed in three-ring binders separated by tabs. When convenient for witness testimony, parties may also use three-ring binders with relevant exhibits separated by witness. Unless otherwise ordered by the Court, the parties shall provide two (2) copies of the exhibit binders to the Court seven (7) days in advance of the motion in limine hearing date.

TRIAL PROCEDURES

Trial generally proceeds from 9:00 a.m. to 5:00 p.m., Tuesday through Friday, unless the Court schedules otherwise. Jury deliberations generally proceed from 9:00 a.m. to 5:00 p.m., unless the Court schedules otherwise.

In civil trials, it is the practice of the Court to set a reasonable time limit for the entire trial. The time limit set by the Court includes opening statements, arguments, testimony, closing arguments and any other matters that occur over the course of the trial, excluding jury selection. The Court will keep track of time limits and upon request, the courtroom deputy will inform the parties of the time spent and remaining for trial. The time limit is subject to exception for good cause shown.

Counsel and witnesses are expected to be present for trial except in case of an emergency. Lawyers must make every effort to have their witnesses available on the day they are to testify. The Court attempts to accommodate witnesses' schedules and may permit counsel to call them out of sequence if warranted. Counsel must anticipate any such possibility and discuss it with opposing counsel and the Court. Counsel must promptly alert the Court to any scheduling problems involving witnesses.

Do not enter the well, except during voir dire, opening statements and closing argument. Conduct all examination of witnesses from the podium. Seek permission from the Court before approaching a witness. Keep your visit to the witness stand brief, i.e., by quickly orienting the witness with an exhibit and returning to the podium. When objecting state only the legal ground for the objection, i.e., "objection, hearsay." Speaking objections are not permitted, unless the Court requests further information from counsel. When a party has more than one lawyer, only one lawyer may conduct the examination of a given witness and that lawyer alone may make objections concerning that witness.

SETTLEMENT

If the parties settle a case, counsel shall immediately notify the magistrate judge of the settlement. If the magistrate judge does not set a deadline for the filing of a "Joint Motion to Dismiss," the parties shall file the "Joint Motion to Dismiss" and email a proposed order to this Court within twenty-eight (28) days of the settlement.

GENERAL DECORUM

All persons, whether observers, witnesses, lawyers, or clients must maintain proper decorum while in the courtroom. Counsel shall rise when addressing the Court, when examining a witness, and, in jury trials, when the jury enters or leaves the courtroom.

B. *Criminal Pretrial and Trial Procedures*

CRIMINAL PRETRIAL AND TRIAL PROCEDURES

Please note: The Court provides this information to counsel and parties for general guidance. Counsel must still strictly adhere to all Court Orders and the Court may vary these procedures as appropriate in any case.

Court Calendar

Criminal Matters are generally heard on Mondays at 9:00a.m. and 2:00p.m. Unless otherwise scheduled by the Court.

Pretrial Motions

Magistrate Judges will schedule the Motion/Trial Setting hearing on the Monday calendar six weeks from the initial appearance before the Magistrate Judge. All motions, except motions in limine and those pertaining to sentencing matters shall be filed at least **21 calendar days** before the hearing date. Opposition briefs shall be filed at least **7 calendar days** before the hearing date.

Applications for an Order Shortening Time are disfavored and must be supported by a non-conclusory affidavit signed by counsel setting forth facts establishing specific good cause.

Disposition Hearings

Rule 11 guilty pleas may be entered before a Magistrate Judge unless the parties anticipate immediate sentencing. Counsel shall contact the courtroom deputy for the Magistrate Judge assigned to the case or the Duty Magistrate Judge to schedule the disposition and immediately inform the courtroom deputy for Judge Hayes of the disposition hearing. *See* Local Rule 11.2.

Trial Procedures

A.   Motions *in Limine*. At the pretrial motions date, the Court will schedule a hearing date for motions *in limine*. Motions *in limine* are due two weeks before the hearing, with any opposition due one week before the hearing.

B.   Trial Briefs. Pursuant to Criminal Local Rule 23.1, the parties may, no later than five court days before the date of trial, serve and file briefs on all significant disputed issues of law, including forseeable procedural and evidentiary issues.

C.   Proposed *Voir Dire* Questions and Verdict Forms. Counsel may serve and file proposed *voir dire* questions and forms of verdict on the day set for motions *in limine*.

D.   Jury Instructions. The parties should each submit proposed jury instructions to the Court on the first day of trial, unless otherwise ordered by the Court. Supplemental instructions must be filed and served as soon as the need for the instruction becomes apparent.

The Court prefers to use the Model Jury Instructions for the Ninth Circuit whenever possible. The Court will accept other proposed jury instructions but counsel must cite the authority supporting the proposed instructions. Any proposed instruction from statutory authority or the Ninth Circuit Model Instructions must state specifically the modification and the authority supporting the modification.

Before the case is submitted to the jury, the Court will provide each party with the jury instructions the Court intends to use. It is each party's responsibility to carefully review the instructions and make suggestions to the Court if modifications appear necessary.

      E.   **Jury Selection.** The Court will conduct the initial *voir dire*. On a case by case basis, the Court may permit follow-up *voir dire* conducted by the attorneys. If *voir dire* is permitted, ten minutes per side on non-complex cases generally will be allowed.

      F.   **Presentation of Evidence.**

- Do not enter the well, except during *voir dire*, opening statements and closing argument.
- Conduct all examination of witnesses from the podium.
- Please seek permission from the Court before approaching a witness.
- Please keep your visit to the witness stand brief, i.e., by quickly orienting the witness with an exhibit and returning to the podium.
- When objecting state only the legal ground for the objection, i.e., "objection, hearsay." Speaking objections are not permitted, unless the Court requests further information from counsel.
- When a party has more than one lawyer, only one lawyer may conduct the examination of a given witness and that lawyer alone may make objections concerning that witness.

      H.   **Exhibits.** Government counsel must provide a list of exhibits and give it to the Courtroom Deputy Clerk on the first day of trial. All exhibits must be pre-marked on the first day of trial. Exhibit stickers may be obtained from the Clerk of the Court or from the Courtroom Deputy Clerk, in advance of trial.

      I.   **Trial Schedule.** Generally, trials are scheduled from 9:00a.m. to 5:00p.m., beginning on Tuesdays. Jury deliberations proceed from 9:00a.m. to 5:00p.m. The Court will notify the parties of deviations from this schedule and will attempt to accommodate jurors, witnesses and counsel, if conflicts arise.

Sentencing

Sentencing procedures are set forth in Criminal Local Rule 32.1. If the parties request, the Court may elect to proceed with immediate sentencing in immigration cases but only where the Court has sufficient information in the record to perform the meaningful exercise of sentencing authority.

      A party seeking a continuance of a sentencing hearing must notify the Courtroom Deputy Clerk at the earliest possible time, but in no event later than noon Friday prior to the Monday sentencing date.

      Counsel shall file the completed sentencing summary chart in the court record or email the sentencing summary chart to "efile_hayes@casd.uscourts.gov" no later than five (5)days before the sentencing hearing required in Criminal Local Rule 32.1 a. 9. Counsel is not required to deliver a copy of the sentencing summary chart to chambers.

General Decorum

All persons, whether observers, witnesses, lawyers, or clients must maintain proper decorum while in the courtroom. Counsel shall rise when addressing the court, when examining a witness, and, in jury trials, when the jury enters or leaves the courtroom.

Hon. John A. Houston
District Judge

Chambers Information
U.S. District Court, Southern District of California
Courtroom 11, 2nd Floor
940 Front Street
San Diego, CA 92101

Scheduling Information
Courtroom Deputy: (619) 557-6424

Biographical Information
Born 1952 in Greensboro, NC

Federal Judicial Service:
- Judge, U. S. District Court, Southern District of California
- Nominated by George W. Bush on May 1, 2003, to a new seat created by 116 Stat. 1758; Confirmed by the Senate on October 2, 2003, and received commission on October 7, 2003.
- U.S. Magistrate Judge, U.S. District Court for the Southern District of California, 1998-2003

Education:
- North Carolina A & T State University, B.S., 1974
- University of Miami at Coral Gables School of Law, J.D., 1977

Professional Career:
- U.S. Army Reserve, 1974-1978, 1981-present
- U.S. Army, Judge Advocate General Corps, 1978-1981
- Assistant U.S. attorney, U.S. Attorney's Office, Southern District of California, 1981-1987
- Chief, Asset Forfeiture Unit, U.S. Attorney's Office, Southern District of California, 1987-1994
- Senior counsel for asset forfeiture, U.S. Attorney's Office, Southern District of California, 1994-1996
- Senior financial litigation counsel, U.S. Attorney's Office, Southern District of California, 1996-1998

Hon. Marilyn L. Huff
District Judge

Chambers Information
U.S. District Court, Southern District of California
Courtroom 13, 5th Floor
940 Front Street
San Diego, CA 92101

Scheduling Information
Courtroom Deputy: (619) 557-6418

Biographical Information
Born 1951 in Ann Arbor, MI

Federal Judicial Service:
- Judge, U. S. District Court, Southern District of California
- Nominated by George H.W. Bush on March 12, 1991, to a seat vacated by William B. Enright; Confirmed by the Senate on May 9, 1991, and received commission on May 14, 1991. Served as chief judge, 1998-2005.

Education:
- Calvin College, B.A., 1972
- University of Michigan Law School, J.D., 1976

Professional Career:
- Private Practice, San Diego, California, 1976-1991

I.   Judge Huff's Procedures and Practices

Judge Huff does not have any specific chambers rules for matters pending before the Court. The Court refers all parties to the applicable federal rules, such as the Federal Rules of Civil Procedure or the Federal Rules of Criminal Procedure, and to the Court's local rules found on the Court's website (http://www.casd.uscourts.gov/index.php?page=local-rules). The Court reserves the right to issue case-specific orders as the need arises.

Hon. M. James Lorenz
District Judge

Chambers Information
U.S. District Court, Southern District of California
Courtroom 14, 5th Floor
940 Front Street
San Diego, CA 92101

Scheduling Information
Courtroom Deputy: (619) 557-6414

Criminal Matters	Mondays at 8:30 a.m. and 2:00 p.m.

Biographical Information
Born 1935 in Pasadena, CA

Federal Judicial Service:
- Judge, U. S. District Court, Southern District of California
- Nominated by William J. Clinton on March 8, 1999, to a seat vacated by Rudi M. Brewster; Confirmed by the Senate on October 1, 1999, and received commission on October 5, 1999. Assumed senior status on October 25, 2009.

Education:
- University of California at Berkeley, B.A., 1957
- California Western School of Law, J.D., 1965

Professional Career:
- Deputy District Attorney, San Diego County District Attorney's Office, CA, 1966-1978
- U.S. Attorney's Office, Southern District of California, 1978-1981
- First Assistant, U.S. Attorney, 1978-1980
- Court Appointed U.S. Attorney, 1980-1981
- Private Practice, San Diego, CA, 1982-1999

I.   **Judge Lorenz's Procedures and Practices**
  A.   *Criminal Pretrial and Trial Procedures*

CRIMINAL PRETRIAL AND TRIAL PROCEDURES

Please note: The Court provides this information to counsel and parties for general guidance. Counsel must still strictly adhere to all Court Orders and the Court may vary these procedures as appropriate in any case.

COURT CALENDAR

Criminal Matters are generally heard on Mondays at 8:30 a.m. and 2:00 p.m. Unless otherwise scheduled by the Court.

PRETRIAL MOTIONS

Magistrate Judges will schedule the motion hearing/trial setting on the Monday calendar four weeks from the initial appearance before the Magistrate Judge. All motions, except motions *in limine* and those pertaining to sentencing matters shall be filed at least **14 calendar days** before the hearing date. Opposition briefs shall be filed at least **7 calendar days** before the hearing date.

Applications for an Order Shortening Time are disfavored and must be supported by a non-conclusory affidavit signed by counsel setting forth facts establishing specific good cause.

Criminal motions requiring a predicate factual finding shall be supported by declaration(s). *See* Crim. LR 47.1(g)(1). The Court need not grant an evidentiary hearing where either party fails to properly support its motion or opposition.

DISPOSITION HEARINGS

Rule 11 guilty pleas may be entered before a Magistrate Judge unless the parties anticipate immediate sentencing. Counsel shall contact the courtroom deputy for the Magistrate Judge assigned to the case or the Duty Magistrate Judge to schedule the disposition. *See* Crim. LR 11.2.

On a related note, all guilty pleas to a lesser offense, superseding information, or less than all counts of the indictment must be entered **2 calendar days** prior to trial unless the Court has been advised. Failure to adhere to this requirement may result in the defendant (or his/her counsel) being assessed the costs of the jury.

EX PARTE REQUESTS

Counsel shall submit an accompanying declaration on **ALL** *ex parte* motions including motions for extraordinary relief. The motion and accompanying declaration must be non-conclusory and must plainly set forth (in detail) the specific reasons for the request.

PROPOSED ORDERS

Parties should submit all proposed orders to the Chamber's e-mail address in WordPerfect format to efile_lorenz@casd.uscourts.gov. Although not encouraged, the Court will accept proposed orders in Word format if necessary.

COURTESY COPIES

Unless otherwise ordered by the Court, parties **MUST** deliver a hard copy of the filing to the Clerk's Office or mail directly to the Chambers, within 24 hours after filing, any criminal case filing which **exceeds 20 pages** in length **including attachments and exhibits**.

In addition, where a party makes multiple filings in a case on the same day, and those filings cumulatively exceed 20 pages, a courtesy copy must be provided to the Court.

If the nature of the filing is such that the need for the Court's immediate attention is anticipated or desired, a courtesy copy **MUST** be delivered <u>on the same day as the filing</u>.

SENTENCING

Sentencing procedures are set forth in Criminal Local Rule 32.1. If the parties request, the Court may elect to proceed with immediate sentencing in immigration cases but only where the Court has sufficient information in the record to perform the meaningful exercise of sentencing authority.

A party seeking a continuance of a sentencing hearing must notify the Courtroom Deputy Clerk at the earliest possible time, <u>but in no event later than **noon Friday**</u> prior to the following week's sentencing date.

Counsel shall file a sentencing summary chart and/or sentencing memorandum **no later than seven (7) days** before the sentencing hearing required in Criminal Local Rule 32.1a.9.

Late filings are unacceptable. All counsel are hereby advised that the filing dates set forth in Criminal Local Rule 32.1 are critical. Absent a showing of good cause, any late filings by counsel may result in a continuance, at minimum. Please be advised that the Court will keep track of such occurrences, and any counsel that repeatedly fails to abide by the timing requirements set forth in Rule 32.1 will be subject to **possible fine or other punitive action** by the Court.

TRIAL PROCEDURES

A.   <u>Motions *in limine*:</u> Motions are due **two weeks before** the hearing, with any opposition due **one week before** the hearing unless otherwise set by the Court.

B.   <u>Trial Briefs:</u> The parties may submit trial briefs no later than **five court days before** the date of trial concerning all significant disputed issues of law, including any and all foreseeable procedural and evidentiary issues with citation of relevant statutes, ordinances, rules, cases and other authorities. *See* Crim. LR 23.1.

C.   <u>*Voir Dire*/Verdict Forms:</u> Counsel may file proposed *voir dire* questions and verdict forms no later than **three court days before** the date of trial.

The Court will conduct the initial *voir dire*. On a case by case basis, the Court may permit follow-up *voir dire* conducted by the attorneys. If *voir dire* is permitted, ten minutes per side will generally be allowed on routine cases.

D.   <u>Proposed Jury Instructions:</u> The parties are encouraged to submit proposed jury instructions to the Court no later than the **first day of trial**, unless otherwise ordered by the Court. Supplemental instructions must be filed as soon as the need for the instruction becomes apparent.

The Court prefers to use the Model Jury Instructions for the Ninth Circuit whenever possible. However, the Court will accept other proposed jury instruction(s) as the need arises, but counsel must cite the authority supporting the proposed instruction(s). Any proposed instruction from statutory authority or the Ninth Circuit Model Instructions must state specifically the modification and the authority supporting the modification.

Before the case is submitted to the jury, the Court will provide each party with the jury instructions the Court intends to use. It is each party's responsibility to carefully review the instructions and make suggestions to the Court if modifications seem necessary.

E.   <u>Presentation of Evidence:</u> Please do not enter the well, except during *voir dire*, opening statements and closing argument. When addressing the jury, do not come any closer than the edge of the Court Reporter's desk. Conduct all examination of witnesses from the podium and please seek permission from the Court before approaching any witness. Also, please keep your visit to the witness stand brief. For example, quickly orient the witness with an exhibit and return to the podium.

F.   <u>Objections:</u> When objecting state only the legal ground for the objection, i.e., "objection, hearsay." Speaking objections are not permitted, unless the Court requests further information from counsel. When a party has more than one lawyer, only one lawyer may conduct the examination of a given witness and that lawyer alone may make objections concerning that witness.

G.   <u>Exhibit Lists:</u> Government counsel must provide a list of exhibits and give it to the Courtroom Deputy Clerk on the **first day of trial**. All exhibits must be pre-marked on the first day of trial. Exhibit stickers may be obtained from the Clerk of the Court or from the Courtroom Deputy Clerk, in advance of trial.

I.   <u>Trial Schedule:</u> In general, criminal trials are scheduled from 9:00 a.m. to 4:30 p.m., beginning on Tuesdays (civil trials may be more flexible. Jury deliberations proceed from 9:00 a.m. to 4:30 p.m. The Court will notify the parties of deviations from this schedule and when possible will attempt to accommodate jurors, witnesses and counsel, should conflicts arise.

B.   *Standing Order for Civil Cases*

STANDING ORDER FOR CIVIL CASES

Except as ordered by the court herein or on a case-by-case basis, all parties shall comply with this District's Local Rules and Electronic Case Filing Administrative Policies and Procedures Manual ("ECF Manual"). Failure to comply with the applicable orders and rules, including the ECF Manual, may result in the noncomplying documents being stricken from the record pursuant to ECF Manual Section 2(a) and sanctions being imposed pursuant to Civil Local Rule 83.1.

Telephone Calls to Chambers

Absent unavoidable circumstances, counsel of record shall personally make any telephone calls to chambers.

Before calling chambers with a procedural question, the caller must familiarize him- or herself with the pertinent rules, including Federal Rules of Civil Procedure, Local Rules of this District, the ECF Manual and the instant Standing Order for Civil Cases.

Court staff is not authorized to interpret orders or give legal advice, including advice on procedural matters.

Courtesy Copies

Courtesy copies of filings exceeding 20 pages shall be delivered directly to chambers.

Unless expressly required by the court, courtesy copies must be identical to the electronically-filed documents.

The pages of each pleading must be firmly bound at the top. In no event shall a courtesy copy of a pleading be delivered unbound.

If a pleading has more than 3 (three) exhibits, the exhibits must be tabbed.

Signature Certification

To meet the signature certification requirement of Section 2(f)(4) of the ECF Manual, the following language must be included when required for joint motions or other documents with multiple signatures: "Pursuant to Section 2(f)(4) of the Electronic Case Filing Administrative Policies and Procedures Manual, I hereby certify that the content of this document is acceptable to [*insert the name of opposing or co-counsel whose electronic signature will be included*], counsel for [*insert name of the party*], and that I have obtained [*Mr./Ms. [name of counsel]*]'s authorization to affix [*his/her*] electronic signature to this document." This statement must be placed under a heading "Signature Certification," located at the end of the document after the signatures, and must be signed by the filing attorney.

Proofs of Service

A proof of service for an electronic filing must be filed as an attachment to the filing in the manner specified in ECF Manual Section 2(g)(2).

Settlement and Dismissal

If a case settles, the parties must immediately notify this court and the assigned Magistrate Judge.

Any joint motion for dismissal of action which includes a provision that the court will retain jurisdiction will be rejected unless: (1) it is accompanied by a fully executed Consent to

Exercise Jurisdiction by a United States Magistrate Judge covering all disputes arising out of the settlement agreement, including interpretation and enforcement of the settlement agreement; and (2) includes in the joint motion and proposed order the following provision: "The Magistrate Judge shall retain jurisdiction over all disputes between and among the parties arising out of the settlement agreement, including but not limited to the interpretation and enforcement of the terms of the settlement agreement.

Ex Parte Applications

Before filing an *ex parte* application, the parties must meet and confer in an attempt to resolve the issue. If the parties are unable to resolve it, the applicant shall attach a declaration documenting the meet and confer efforts and explain the reason for failure to reach a resolution, or explain why a meeting and conference is not appropriate in the context of the request.

The court will rule upon simple administrative requests without requiring a response from the opposing party. If a party intends to oppose, the party must immediately contact chambers and request an opportunity to file an opposition.

Proposed Orders

Although the ECF Manual permits lodging proposed orders in Word, this court prefers and strongly encourages parties to submit them in WordPerfect instead.

All extraneous information (i.e., attorney and firm name, headers, footers and watermarks) must be removed from the proposed order.

Motions to Seal Documents

Before attempting to file any document under seal, a party must file an *ex parte* application to obtain leave of court.

Motion Briefing

When the same party is noticing multiple motions for the same hearing date, the motions must be briefed together in one memorandum of points and authorities.

If multiple parties are moving for substantially the same relief, they shall make every effort to obtain the same hearing date for their motions.

If multiple parties are moving for substantially the same relief, or opposing a motion seeking substantially the same relief sought against them, noticed for the same hearing date, counsel shall make every effort to coordinate and consolidate the briefing or use the notice of joinder procedure so as to avoid duplication in briefing. If the briefing is not coordinated or consolidated, counsel for each party must file an affidavit concurrently with the briefing describing the efforts and explaining why they were not successful.

Summary Judgment Motions and Cross-Motions

If upon being served with a summary judgment motion an opposing party determines that it intends to file a cross-motion, the party must contact chambers well in advance of the due date for the opposition to the first-filed summary judgment motion.

Any separate statements of disputed or undisputed facts will be rejected.

Ten days before the hearing date, the parties shall meet and confer in person to arrive at a joint statement of undisputed facts, which shall be filed no later than the reply brief.

Motions to Reconsider

Motions to reconsider may be filed without first obtaining a hearing date from chambers. The memorandum of points and authorities in support of the motion shall be no more than ten (10) pages in length. If the court finds the motion merits further briefing, a scheduling order will issue.

Memoranda of Contentions of Fact and Law

This court does not require memoranda of contentions of fact and law.

Trial Briefs

This court does not require trial briefs for the cases or issues tried to the jury.

Motions *in Limine*

The hearing date and briefing schedule for motions *in limine* will be set in the order issued after the final pretrial conference.

Before filing any motions *in limine*, the parties must meet and confer in person in an attempt to resolve the issues. If the parties are unable to resolve them, the moving party shall attach a declaration documenting the meet and confer efforts and explain the reason for failure to reach a resolution.

Parties must not present summary judgment motions or motions to dismiss under the label of motions *in limine*. Any such motions must be filed within the time provided in the case management order.

Parties are encouraged to be selective with their motions *in limine* and not to file mundane, boilerplate or unnecessary motions.

Exhibits

The parties shall avoid duplication of exhibits as much as possible. If the same exhibit is referred to in more than one motion noticed for the same day, the exhibit should be filed only once. Similarly, if both sides refer to the same exhibit relative to a motion noticed for the same day, only one side should file the exhibit. The parties shall use citations to assist the court in locating such exhibits.

Interpreters and Translations

It is the sole responsibility of the party presenting foreign language testimony to arrange for an interpreter. Well in advance of calling the witness, the party shall file a stipulation showing that the parties agree to the interpreter or a declaration showing that the interpreter is court-approved.

Any foreign language exhibits must be accompanied by a translation together with a stipulation that the parties agree to the translation or a declaration showing that the document was translated by a court-approved translator.

Audio and Video Exhibits

Any party relying on audio or video exhibits in motion briefing, at a hearing or at trial, must simultaneously file or introduce a transcript of the exhibit. The transcript shall either be certified by a court reporter or stipulated to by the opposing party.

Electronic, Audio and Video Equipment

Parties shall notify the courtroom deputy at least five (5) court days before a hearing or trial of any electronic, audio or video equipment they intend to use in the courtroom and jointly prepare and lodge a proposed order seeking leave to use the equipment in the courtroom. The proposed order shall itemize all equipment and list the dates when it will be used in court. The order must be presented to the security personnel when the equipment is brought into the courthouse.

Trial Exhibits

Trial exhibits must be pre-marked. Any questions regarding marking trial exhibits shall be directed to the Courtroom Deputy.

Hon. Jeffrey T. Miller
District Judge

Chambers Information
U.S. District Court, Southern District of California
Courtroom 16, 5th Floor
940 Front Street
San Diego, CA 92101

Scheduling Information
Courtroom Deputy: (619) 557-7439

Civil Law and Motion	Mondays at 10:00 a.m.
Criminal Matters	First and Third Fridays of each month at 9:00 a.m.

Biographical Information
Born 1943 in New York, NY

Federal Judicial Service:
- Judge, U. S. District Court, Southern District of California
- Nominated by William J. Clinton on January 7, 1997, to a seat vacated by Gordon Thompson, Jr.; Confirmed by the Senate on May 23, 1997, and received commission on May 27, 1997.

Education:
- University of California, Los Angeles, B.A., 1964
- University of California, Los Angeles, School of Law, J.D., 1967

Professional Career:
- Deputy State Attorney General, California, 1968-1987
- Judge, California Superior Court, San Diego County, 1987-1997

I.   **Judge Miller's Procedures and Practices**
       A.   *Standing Rules for Civil Matters*

STANDING RULES FOR CIVIL MATTERS

These rules are designed to assist attorneys or parties appearing pro se before Judge Miller in civil matters. They answer many commonly received questions and explain procedures that are specific to Judge Miller's chambers. To reach Judge Miller's Judicial Assistant or one of his law clerks, please call 619-557-6627.

I.   *General Calendaring Information*

Except as otherwise provided herein or as specifically ordered by the Court, all parties are expected to strictly comply with this District's Local Rules. The Local Rules of Practice for the Southern District of California can be found on the Court's website: Http://www.casd.circ9.dcn/index.php?page=local-rules.

Civil motions are generally scheduled on ***Mondays beginning at 10:00 a.m.*** Judge Miller's civil calendar is set and maintained by his law clerks. When seeking to set or continue a civil motion, counsel should first contact the law clerk assigned to the case. If you are instructed to e-file a joint motion to continue the hearing date, ***remember to submit a proposed order simultaneously to efile_miller@casd.uscourts.gov.*** Proposed Orders must be submitted in Word Perfect or Word format. Any request for a continuance must be timely made under the circumstances.

Discovery matters and Settlement Conferences are handled by the assigned magistrate judge. The parties shall contact the appropriate magistrate judge's chambers to calendar hearings in discovery matters and settlement conferences.

II.   *Communication with the Court*

Telephone Calls. Telephone calls to chambers are permitted ONLY for matters such as docketing, scheduling, or calendaring. Court personnel are prohibited from giving legal advice or discussing the merits of a case. When calling chambers, be prepared to identify your case as odd or even based on the last digit of the case number (i.e., 09cv1234 is an even-numbered case, 08cv2345 is an odd-numbered case), so your call can be directed to the appropriate law clerk.

Document submissions. Please refer to the Local Rules for a complete list of deadlines and compliance requirements. http://www.casd.circ9.dcn/index.php?page=local-rules. Except as otherwise provided herein, or as specifically ordered by the Court, all parties are expected to strictly comply with this District's Local Rules.

The Electronic Case Filing Administrative Policies & Procedures Manual can be found on the Court's website at: Http://www.casd.uscourts.gov/index.pho?page=attorney-assistance.

Courtesy copies of e-filed documents longer than 20 pages, including exhibits, MUST be submitted to chambers. Failure to submit courtesy copies may result in a continuance of the hearing.

Faxes. Faxes to chambers are **prohibited** unless specifically requested by the Court. If faxes are requested, copies of the same shall be simultaneously faxed or delivered to all counsel. Contact chambers for the fax number.

Letters. Letters and other ex parte communications which relate to a case shall not be sent to chambers unless specifically requested by the Court. Copies of correspondence between counsel shall not be sent to the Court. If letters are requested by the Court, copies of the same shall be simultaneously delivered to all counsel. Requested correspondence should be addressed as follows:

Jeffrey T. Miller, United States District Judge
Southern District Of California
Edward J. Schwartz U.S. Courthouse
940 Front Street, Room 5190
San Diego, California 92101-8917

III. *Noticed Motions*

Hearing Dates. Counsel shall obtain all hearing dates from the appropriate law clerk before filing moving papers. Any hearing dates for motions to be heard before Judge Miller scheduled by the magistrate judge assigned to the case shall be confirmed with the appropriate law clerk before the parties file their moving papers. *Moving papers MUST be filed and served within 3 days of obtaining a motion hearing date from chambers.*

Oral Argument. Although the Court often decides motions based on the papers submitted by the parties, it is the Court's policy to schedule oral argument for dispositive motions or when all counsel request oral argument. Counsel will be notified by the law clerk assigned to the matter once the decision is made as to whether oral argument is needed to assist in deciding a given motion. The Court endeavors to make the decision as to whether oral argument will be scheduled as early as possible. In the event the moving party desires to submit on the papers, the phrase "No Oral Argument Requested" should appear on the caption.

Points and Authorities. In their memoranda of points and authorities, the parties shall state all legal and factual bases for the motion in the opening brief. Factual matters or legal arguments raised by a party for the first time in their reply brief, unless directly in response to the opposition, may not be considered.

Statement of Non-Opposition, Failure to Oppose. A party that determines that it will not oppose a given motion shall file a statement of non-opposition no later than 14 days before the hearing date. An opposing party's failure to file a memorandum of points and authorities in opposition to any motion will be construed as consent to the granting of the motion.

Motions for Reconsideration. Motions for reconsideration are disfavored unless a party shows there is new evidence, a change in controlling law, or establishes that the Court committed a clear error in the earlier ruling.

IV. *Ex Parte Motions*

Ex parte applications are not subject to the scheduling requirements of Civ.L.R. 7.1 and do not require the parties to obtain a hearing date from chambers prior to filing the application. There are two broad categories of relief appropriate for resolution by ex parte application. The first category encompasses requests for simple administrative relief such as requests to enlarge time, shorten time, exceed the page limitations, etc. The second category encompasses requests for expedited substantive relief such as requests for temporary restraining orders to freeze assets for seizure of infringing goods, etc.

Requests for Administrative Relief. In the majority of cases, the court will rule upon simple administrative requests within 48 hours without requesting a response from the opposing party. The court will not consider any administrative request that has not been served on the opposing party. In the event a party opposes the application, the party must contact chambers immediately and request the opportunity to submit a response.

Requests for Substantive Relief without Notice. True ex parte relief (that is, a request for relief without notice to the opposing party) is rarely appropriate unless authorized by statute. True ex parte relief is subject to the requirements of Fed.R.Civ.P. 65 and Civ.L.R. 83.3(h). Upon filing a motion for true ex parte relief, the proponent must immediately contact chambers and request a hearing. Chambers staff will inform the proponent of any additional procedures applicable to the party's request.

Requests for Substantive Relief with Notice. Where a party requests a temporary restraining order or the application of a state law remedy encompassed within the scope of Fed.R.Civ.P. 64 or 69, notice must be provided to all interested parties. Upon filing the motion, the proponent shall immediately inform chambers that a motion for expedited relief has been filed with the court. The proponent shall provide chambers with the identity of opposing counsel and contact information. Pursuant to chambers policy, staff will contact the opposing party and request a response and, given the nature of the request, may also request a reply brief and/or set the matter for oral argument.

V. *Continuances*

Parties requesting a continuance of any conference, scheduled motion, hearing date, deadline, or briefing schedule or other procedural change shall meet and confer prior to contacting the Court. If the parties reach an agreement, they shall e-file a joint motion with a detailed declaration of the reason for the requested continuance or extension of time. They shall also e-mail a proposed Order to efile_miller@casd.uscourts.gov. Except in extraordinary circumstances, joint motions to amend a briefing schedule or to continue a motion hearing date must be filed no later than three court days before the affected date. If the parties are unable to reach an agreement, the requesting party shall file an ex parte application satisfying the applicable legal standard, with a particular focus on the diligence of the party seeking delay and any prejudice that may result therefrom. In addition, the ex parte application shall state (1) the original hearing date, (2) the number of previous continuance requests, and (3) whether previous requests were granted or denied.

VI. *Proposed Orders*

Proposed orders must be submitted simultaneously with the filing of all joint motions or ex parte requests. The proposed order should be emailed to efile_miller@casd.uscourts.gov *in WordPerfect* or Word format. All extraneous information (i.e., attorney and firm name, headers, footers, and watermarks) should be removed from the proposed order. If possible, the docket number of the corresponding motion should be included in the caption. The proposed order should be named as follows: case number_title_date (e.g., 00cv1234_order granting continuance_5 6 09).

IN THE UNITED STATES DISTICT COURT
FOR THE SOUTHERN DISTRICT OF CALIFORNIA

SMITH,
      Plaintiff,

     v.

JONES,
      Defendant.

)
)
)
)
)
)
)
)

Civil No. 00cv1234 JM(KCA)

**Order Granting Joint Motion to Continue
Motion Hearing [Docket No. 12]**

IT IS SO ORDERED.

VII. _Pre-trial Conferences_

Parties shall submit the Proposed Pretrial Order as required by the Civil Local Rules by the date indicated in the Scheduling Order issued by the magistrate judge assigned to the matter. The parties are NOT required to submit a Memorandum of Contentions of Fact and Law as set forth in Civ. L.R. 16.1(f)(2).

VIII. _Motions in Limine_

Motions _in Limine_ may be heard the Friday before trial is scheduled to begin or the morning of the first day of trial prior to jury impanelment. The judge will assign a Motions _in Limine_ date at the time of the Pretrial Conference. Before filing any motions _in limine_, parties are required to meet and confer in person in an attempt to resolve their dispute. If the parties are unable to resolve their differences, counsel filing the motion _in limine_ shall attach a declaration documenting the parties' meet-and-confer efforts and the reason for their unsuccessful efforts. Parties are encouraged to be selective with their motions _in limine_ and not to file mundane or unnecessary motions.

IX. _Trials_

Trials are generally scheduled Monday through Thursday, 9 a.m. to 12 noon and 1:30 p.m. - 4:30 p.m. Trial briefs should be filed no later than 5 calendar days before trial is to commence in all cases and shall include proposed voir dire questions to be asked by counsel and/or the Court.

Jury Instructions. Judge Miller prefers to use the Ninth Circuit Civil Jury Instructions when possible. ***Proposed jury instructions should be filed by both sides one week prior to the commencement of trial.*** The final jury instructions will be issued by Judge Miller after discussion with counsel.

Jury Selection. The courtroom deputy will provide counsel with a numerical list of the jury panel along with a seating chart. Generally, Judge Miller seats 20-25 prospective jurors and permits counsel to voir dire after the Court's extensive voir dire and after the prospective jurors have answered a short questionnaire.

Exhibits. Counsel are required to premark exhibits with all exhibits designated as Court Exhibits. Please contact Judge Miller's courtroom deputy, Gabriela Cazares at 619-557-7439 for specific information. All trial exhibits are returned to counsel at the conclusion of trial.

X.   *Miscellaneous Procedures*

If a witness requires an interpreter, it is counsel's responsibility to notify the clerk or interpreter section, in advance, of the need for an interpreter for a witness. Counsel shall refrain from using foreign languages on the record in court. The Court Reporter reports only in English.

Where a party has more than one lawyer, only one may object during direct or cross-examination of a given witness.

B.   *Standing Rules for Criminal Matters*

STANDING RULES FOR CRIMINAL MATTERS

These rules are designed to assist attorneys or parties appearing pro se before Judge Miller in criminal matters. They answer many commonly received questions and explain procedures that are specific to Judge Miller's chambers. To reach Judge Miller's Judicial Assistant or one of his law clerks, please call 619-557-6627.

I.   *General Calendaring Information*

A. Criminal matters, including sentencings, motions, revocation proceedings, and status hearings are generally scheduled on the *1st and 3rd Fridays* of each month, beginning at *9:00 a.m.*

B. Judge Miller's criminal calendar is set and maintained by his Courtroom Deputy, Gabriela Cazares. Ms. Cazares can be reached at 619-557-7439.

C. When seeking a continuance, counsel should first contact Ms. Cazares. If you are instructed to e-file a joint motion to continue the hearing date, **remember to submit a proposed order simultaneously to** *efile_miller@casd.uscourts.gov.* Proposed Orders must be submitted in Word Perfect or Word format. Any request must be timely made under the circumstances.

II.   *Document Submissions*

A. Please refer to the Local Rules for a complete list of deadlines and compliance requirements. http://www.casd.circ9.dcn/index.php?page=local-rules.

B. Motions for Orders Shortening Time are unnecessary!

C. The Electronic Case Filing Administrative Policies & Procedures Manual can bevfound on the Court's website at: http://www.casd.uscourts.gov/cmecf/pdf/CASDPolicies.pdf. *Courtesy copies of e-filed documents related to criminal matters need not be submitted unlessvspecifically requested by Judge Miller's Judicial Assistant.*

D. **Sentencing Memoranda and Sentencing Summary Charts** should be filed *5 court days (usually 7 calendar days)* prior to the scheduled hearing. *If they are late, do not file a Motion for an Order Shortening Time.*

E. **Motions** should be filed 14 days prior to the hearing and responses and oppositions should be filed 7 days prior to the hearing.

F. **Letters.** Letters and other ex parte communication to chambers are prohibited unless specifically requested by the Court. Copies of correspondence between counsel shall not be sent to the Court. If letters are requested by the Court, copies of the same shall be simultaneously delivered to all counsel. Requested correspondence should be addressed as follows:

Jeffrey T. Miller, United States District Judge
Edward J. Schwartz U.S. Courthouse
940 Front Street, Room 5190
San Diego, California 92101-8917

G. **Faxes.** Faxes to chambers are **prohibited** unless specifically requested by the Court. If faxes are requested, copies of the same shall be simultaneously faxed or delivered to all counsel. Call chambers at 619-557-6627 for permission to fax a document and to get the fax number.

III. _Rule 11 Guilty Pleas_

Unless the parties anticipate immediate sentencing, the Court directs **all** Rule 11 guilty pleas to be entered before a magistrate judge.

IV. _Trials_

1. Trials are generally scheduled Monday through Thursday, 9 a.m. to 12 noon and 1:30 p.m. to 4:30 p.m.

2. Motions _in Limine_ may be heard the Friday before the trial is scheduled to begin or the morning of the first day of trial prior to jury impanelment.

3. Trial briefs should be filed no later than 5 calendar days before trial is to commence in cases where there is any significant disputed issue of law, or if a party is requesting that specific questions be asked or specific topics be covered during the Court's voir dire. Proposed voir dire, whether to be asked by counsel or proposed for the Court to ask, must be submitted in written form no later than 7 days prior to commencement of trial.

A. Jury

1) Jury Instructions: Judge Miller prefers to use the Ninth Circuit Criminal Jury Instructions when possible. ***Proposed jury instructions should be submitted by both sides no later than 5 calendar days prior to the commencement of trial.***

2) Jury Selection: The courtroom deputy will provide counsel with a numerical list of the jury panel along with a seating chart. Generally, Judge Miller seats 32 prospective jurors and permits counsel to voir dire after the Court's extensive voir dire and jurors have answered a short jury questionnaire. Counsel exercise their peremptory challenges utilizing separate strike sheets.

B. Exhibits

1) Counsel are requested to pre-mark exhibits with plaintiff/government counsel using numbers and defense using letters.

2) Government counsel shall provide a list of exhibits to the courtroom deputy on the first day of trial.

3) All trial exhibits are returned to counsel at the conclusion of

trial.

C. Miscellaneous Procedures

1) It is defense counsel's responsibility to arrange for an in-custody criminal defendant to be dressed in appropriate clothing ahead of time, consistent with the procedures at the institution where the defendant is being housed.

2) If the defendant and/or a witness requires an interpreter, it is counsel's responsibility to notify the interpreter section, in advance, of the need for an interpreter. Counsel shall refrain from using foreign languages on the record in court. The Court Reporter reports only in English.

3) Where a party has more than one lawyer, only one may object during direct or cross-examination of a given witness.

Hon. Barry Ted Moskowitz
Chief District Judge

Chambers Information
U.S. District Court, Southern District of California
Courtroom 15, 5th Floor
940 Front Street
San Diego, CA 92101

Scheduling Information
Courtroom Deputy: (619) 557-5492

Biographical Information
Born 1950 in Patterson, NJ

Federal Judicial Service:
- Judge, U. S. District Court, Southern District of California
- Nominated by William J. Clinton on June 30, 1995, to a new seat created by 104 Stat. 5089; Confirmed by the Senate on December 22, 1995, and received commission on December 26, 1995. Served as chief judge, 2012-present.
- U.S. Magistrate, U.S. District Court for the Southern District of California, 1986-1995

Education:
- Rutgers College, B.A., 1972
- Rutgers University School of Law, J.D., 1975

Professional Career:
- Law Clerk, U.S. Court of Appeals, Third Circuit, 1975-1976
- Assistant U.S. Attorney, District of New Jersey, 1976-1982
- Private Practice, Wayne, New Jersey, 1982-1985
- Assistant U.S. Attorney, Southern District of California, 1985-1988

I.   **Judge Moskowitz's Procedures and Practices**
    A.   Order Limiting Submission of Sentencing Materials

IN THE UNITED STATES DISTICT COURT
FOR THE SOUTHERN DISTRICT OF CALIFORNIA

IN RE:	)	NO. _____
	)	
LIMITATION OF SENTENCING	)	**ORDER**
MATERIALS IN CASES ASSIGNED	)	
TO JUDGE MOSKOWITZ	)	
_____	)	

IT IS HEREBY ORDERED that no party in a criminal case shall submit more than five (5) letters unless authorized by the court for good cause shown.

Additional letters may be submitted to the probation officer who is preparing the presentence report for summarization in the report. Counsel may also submit to the court as part of a sentencing memorandum a brief summary of letters in excess of the amount authorized by this order. Any letters submitted to the court must be filed no later than three (3) days prior to sentencing. The court's staff shall strike from the record any letters filed or submitted in violation of this order and they shall not be made available to the court for review.

Thus, any letters submitted in violation of this chamber's order shall not be read by the court or be part of the record.

IT IS SO ORDERED.

DATED: October 31, 2001

FILED: November 5, 2001

Hon. Dana M. Sabraw
District Judge

Chambers Information
U.S. District Court, Southern District of California
Courtroom 10, 2nd Floor
940 Front Street
San Diego, CA 92101

Scheduling Information
Courtroom Deputy: (619) 557-6399

Criminal Law and Motion	Fridays at 11:00 a.m.

Biographical Information
Born 1958 in San Rafael, CA

Federal Judicial Service:
- Judge, U. S. District Court, Southern District of California
- Nominated by George W. Bush on May 1, 2003, to a new seat created by 116 Stat. 1758; Confirmed by the Senate on September 25, 2003, and received commission on September 26, 2003.

Education:
- American River Junior College, A.A., 1978
- San Diego State University, B.S., 1980
- University of the Pacific, McGeorge School of Law, J.D., 1985

Professional Career:
- Private Practice, San Diego, California, 1985-1989
- Private Practice, Santa Barbara, California, 1989-1995
- Judge, North County Municipal Court, County of San Diego, California, 1995-1998
- Judge, Superior Court for the State of California, County of San Diego, California, 1998-2003

I.   Judge Sabraw's Procedures and Practices
A.   *Civil Pretrial and Trial Procedures*

Civil Pretrial and Trial Procedures of Judge Dana M. Sabraw

Unless otherwise ordered, matters before Judge Sabraw shall be conducted in accordance with the following practices:

1.   Communications with Chambers.
A.   Letters. Letters to chambers are prohibited, unless specifically requested by the Court. If letters are requested, copies of the same shall be simultaneously delivered to all counsel. Copies of correspondence between counsel shall not be sent to the Court.

B.   Faxes. Faxes to chambers are prohibited, unless specifically requested by the Court. If faxes are requested, copies of the same shall be simultaneously faxed or delivered to all counsel. Pleadings that are filed with the Clerk's Office may be faxed to chambers, provided that copies are simultaneously faxed or delivered to all counsel. Do not follow with a hard copy. The chambers fax number is 619-702-9942.

C.   Telephone Calls. Telephone calls to chambers are permitted only for matters such as docketing, scheduling or calendaring. Court personnel are prohibited from giving legal advice or discussing the merits of a case. Call chambers at 619-557-6262, and address your inquiries to the Law Clerks.

2.   Temporary Restraining Orders/Preliminary Injunctions. Temporary restraining orders and preliminary injunctions will issue pursuant to Rule 65 of the Federal Rules of Civil Procedure. While temporary restraining orders may be heard *ex parte*, the Court may in its discretion order service on the opposing party before proceeding. Alternatively, a limited temporary restraining order may issue to preserve the *status quo* pending further briefing. The Court generally will provide telephonic notice of the date and time of any hearing.

3.   Early Neutral Evaluation Conference. Pursuant to Civil Local Rule 16.1.c, within 45 days of the filing of an answer, counsel and the parties shall appear before the magistrate judge supervising discovery for an early neutral evaluation ("ENE") conference. If a Rule 12(b) motion is filed instead of an answer, and the motion is granted with leave to amend, the Court may in its discretion order the parties to an ENE conference before an answer is filed and while briefing on the amended complaint is pending. *See* Fed.R.Civ.P. 16(b).

The appearance at the ENE conference shall be made with authority to discuss and enter into settlement, and if no settlement is reached, to set pretrial and trial dates. The parties should consult with the magistrate judge to determine if any special procedures exist for conducting the ENE conference.

If no settlement is reached at the ENE conference, a case management conference ("CMC") will be held within 30 days after the ENE conference. In the discretion of the magistrate judge, the CMC may be held at the ENE conference.

4.   Case Management Conference and Trial Setting. Prior to the CMC all counsel shall discuss discovery issues and endeavor to resolve any disputes. Procedures for the CMC are set forth in Civil Local Rule 16.1.d. In consultation with the parties, the magistrate judge shall determine at the CMC whether the case is to be deemed complex. For non-complex and complex cases, the following procedures will apply:

A. **Non-Complex Cases.** A case management order will issue following the CMC and after consultation with the magistrate judge. The order will set forth a discovery schedule and cut-off dates, including, if applicable, expert witness disclosure and discovery dates, a pretrial motions cutoff date, a pretrial conference date, and a trial date.

Pretrial dates generally will be set in accordance with the following schedule: (1) ENE conference within 45 days after filing of an answer (or in the Court's discretion within 45 days after an Order granting Rule 12(b) motion with leave to amend); (2) CMC within 30 days after ENE conference; (3) discovery cut-off within seven months after CMC; (4) pretrial motion cut-off within four weeks after discovery cut-off; (5) pretrial conference within four months after motion cut-off, and (6) trial date within six weeks after pretrial conference.

Trial dates, in accordance with Civil Local Rule 16.5.c, will be set within 18 months of the filing of the complaint. Specifically, trial dates will be set within: (1) 12 months of the filing of the complaint in cases involving social security, enforcement of judgments, forfeiture, and prisoner petitions challenging conditions of confinement; (2) 15 months of the filing of the complaint in FTCA cases; and (3) 18 months of the filing of the complaint in all other cases not deemed to be complex. A trial date may be set by the magistrate judge beyond the dates specified above for good cause shown.

B. **Complex and Class Action Cases.**

(1) **Non-Class Action Complex Cases.** In non-class action complex cases, a trial date will be set within 24 months of the CMC, in the absence of good cause shown for a later date. All other pretrial dates will be adjusted in accordance with the trial date.

(2) **Class Action Cases.** At the conclusion of the ENE, the magistrate judge will discuss with the parties class certification, discovery regarding class certification, the appointment of class counsel if that matter has not already been addressed, any contemplated pre-certification motions for summary judgment, and related issues. Thereafter, the magistrate judge will issue either at the ENE or CMC a schedule for the class certification motion, or, if appropriate, a schedule for a pre-certification dispositive motion. A trial date also will be set. The trial date will be set within 24 months of the CMC, in the absence of good cause shown for a later date.

In cases not involving a pre-certification dispositive motion, a discovery and briefing schedule for class certification will be set. Generally, the class certification motion will be heard within 90 days of the CMC, and discovery regarding the motion will not be parsed between "class" and "merits" discovery, provided, however, that the magistrate judge may in his or her discretion set other dates or discovery provisions that are tailored to the needs of the case.

In cases where a pre-certification dispositive motion is deemed to be appropriate, the magistrate judge will set a discovery and briefing schedule in consultation with the parties. Such motions generally will be heard within 90 days of the CMC, in the absence of good cause shown for a later date.

C. **All Cases.** The pretrial motions cut-off date is the last date on which motions may be filed. Motion hearings are generally scheduled at least 35 days from the time the motion is filed. Please be mindful of these rules when calling to reserve a hearing date.

5.   Discovery Disputes. All motions to compel discovery are referred to the magistrate judge assigned to the case. Motions pursuant to Rules 26 through 37 of the Federal Rules of Civil Procedure will not be heard unless the parties previously have met and conferred concerning all disputed issues. Civ. L.R. 26.1.a. The parties should consult the magistrate judge assigned to the case for any special procedures regarding discovery issues.

6.   Motions.

A.   Rule 12(b) Motions: Informal Conference. Any party desiring to file a Rule 12(b) motion shall first attempt to resolve the matter informally. If no informal resolution is achieved, the moving party shall contact the Court's Law Clerk to obtain a date for an in-chambers conference (in person or telephonic), and arrange for the opposing party to appear at that time. The moving party shall, no later than two days before the conference, fax to chambers and serve on the opposing party an informal statement explaining why such motion is warranted. No statement is required of the opposing party. The time prescribed by the Federal Rules of Civil Procedure for the moving party's first responsive pleading shall be tolled until after the conference. At the conclusion of the conference, the parties may stipulate to allow the filing of an amended complaint, or, in the absence of a stipulation, the moving party shall be permitted to file and serve a Rule 12(b) motion within a reasonable period of time, to be set at the conference.

B.   Motions Generally: Scheduling a Hearing Date. Pursuant to Civil Local Rule 7.1.b, all dates for motion hearings must be obtained by calling the Law Clerk. Briefing schedules are set forth in the Local Rules. There are no additional filing deadlines, unless the Court sets a specific briefing schedule in the case. A hearing date will not be reserved unless the motion is filed on the date on which the Law Clerk is contacted to schedule the hearing date. Motion hearing dates generally are set within 30 to 60 days from the date the motion is filed, depending upon the nature and complexity of the motion.

C.   Oral Argument. At the Court's discretion, motions will be decided on the papers and without oral argument, in accordance with Civil Local Rule 7.1.d.1. If the motion is to be decided without oral argument, counsel will be notified by order of the Court canceling oral argument at least five days before the scheduled hearing date. In the absence of such an order, oral argument will proceed on the assigned hearing date. The Court generally reserves oral argument for matters that are either procedurally significant or dispositive, and may issue a tentative ruling before the hearing date. Oral argument will occur on the Court's Friday Calendar at 1:30 p.m. Telephonic argument is permitted in the Court's discretion, provided arrangements are made in advance of the hearing. Civ. L.R. 7.1.d.3.

D.   Courtesy Copies. Courtesy copies of pleadings, marked as such, shall be submitted to chambers, as soon as practicable after filing.

E.   Proposed Orders. In accordance with Section 2(h) of the Electronic Case Filing Administrative Policies and Procedures Manual, counsel shall e-mail proposed orders on motions directly to the Judge's official e-mail address, which is efile_sabraw@casd.uscourts.gov. Proposed orders should be submitted simultaneously with the motion.

7.   Pretrial Conference.

        A.   Matters Covered. Pursuant to Civil Local Rule 16.1.f.6, the Court requires the plaintiff to lodge a pretrial order no less than five days before the pretrial conference. The pretrial order must include all matters set out in Civil Local Rule 16.1.f.6.c and any other issues relevant to the trial. Counsel shall be prepared to discuss scheduling, time limits, jury selection (if applicable), settlement, consent to magistrate judge jurisdiction for trial, and all other issues related to trial. Pretrial conferences are held on the Court's Friday Calendar at 10:30 a.m.

        B.   Motions *in Limine* and Other Exchange Dates. A briefing schedule for motions *in limine* will be set at the pretrial conference, along with dates by which to file a final list of witnesses and exhibits, and – in jury cases – proposed *voir dire* questions, jury instructions, verdict forms, and a joint statement of the case to be read to the jury. The Court also will set reasonable time limits for the trial in consultation with counsel at the pretrial conference.

8.   Trial Procedures.

        A.   Motions *in Limine*. Generally, motions *in limine* will be heard one to two weeks before trial. Such motions must be filed and served two weeks before the scheduled hearing date, with oppositions due one week before the hearing. No reply briefs are permitted.

        B.   Jury Instructions. Jury instructions shall be submitted to the Court one week before trial in the following format:

                (1)   The parties are required **jointly** to submit one set of agreed upon instructions. To this end, the parties shall meet and confer, and thereafter submit to the Court one complete set of agreed upon instructions. The Court prefers to use standard pattern instructions, such as the Ninth Circuit Model Jury Instructions, Civil, the California Civil Jury Instructions (CACI), or other pattern instructions from other states, if applicable.

                (2)   If the parties cannot agree upon one complete set of instructions, they are required to submit one set of instructions to which they have agreed, and two sets (one for each party) of supplemental instructions to which they have not agreed.

                (3)   The joint instructions and supplemental instructions must be presented to the Court one week before trial, along with any objections to the supplemental instructions. All objections to supplemental instructions shall be in writing, set forth the challenged jury instruction **in its entirety,** identify the objectionable language, and contain citation to authority explaining why the instruction is improper. Where applicable, the objecting party shall submit an alternative instruction.

                (4)   The parties are required to submit the proposed joint set of instructions and proposed supplemental instructions in the following format:

                        (a)   Two copies of each instruction should be provided.

                        (b)   The first copy should indicate the number of the proposed instruction, the instruction, and the authority supporting the instruction.

                        (c)   The second copy should contain **only** the proposed instructions on plain paper, that is, not on pleading paper. No other marks or writings should be present. This copy also should be presented on a floppy disk in WordPerfect format (any version).

(5)   All instructions should be short, concise, and neutral statements of law.

(6)   Any modification to a standard instruction must be identified by specifying the modification to the original instruction and the authority supporting the modification.

C.   Trial Briefs. Pursuant to Civil Local Rule 16.1.f.9, the parties shall, no later than 7 days before the date of trial, serve and file briefs on all significant disputed issues of law, including foreseeable procedural and evidentiary issues.

D.   Proposed *Voir Dire* Questions/Jury Questionnaire and Verdict Forms. The parties shall submit proposed *voir dire* questions and verdict forms one week before trial. The Court also will consider a jury questionnaire if requested at the pretrial conference, and approved by the Court.

E.   Jury Selection. The following is a description of the struck panel method by which the jury will be selected. There are many variations on this basic technique, so it is important that counsel understand what procedure will be followed. The procedure may require counsel to take more careful notes and to observe more panelists than under some traditional jury box selection methods.

The Courtroom Deputy Clerk will provide counsel with a numerical list of the jury panel at the beginning of *voir dire*, along with a seating chart. Jurors assigned seat numbers one through fourteen will be questioned.

The number of jurors questioned (fourteen) is calculated as follows: the number of jurors to be selected (generally eight) plus the number of peremptory challenges (generally six or three per side). Thus, *voir dire* will be conducted from fourteen panelists for the usual eight-person jury. If there is to be a ten-person jury, two additional panelists will be added.

The Court will conduct the initial jury *voir dire*. On a case by case basis, the Court may permit follow-up *voir dire* conducted by counsel. If *voir dire* is permitted, fifteen minutes per side on noncomplex cases generally will be allowed.

After the Court and counsel have *voir dired* the panel, counsel may exercise challenges for cause. If any challenges for cause are sustained, the removed panelists will be replaced by inserting new panelists from the *venire* so that a full panel exists before any peremptory challenges are exercised. The new panelists will be *voir dired* in accordance with the above.

The exercise of peremptory challenges will follow. Counsel will exercise alternating challenges – generally outside the presence of the prospective jurors – by calling out the jurors' numbers they wish to excuse. The process will be repeated until all peremptory challenges are exhausted.

Note that a party may waive its right to challenge but may not reserve. Thus, if counsel passes one time, he or she may not exercise any more peremptory challenges. Also note that challenges may be made to any of the panelists regardless where that panelist appears in the array.

When each side has exhausted its peremptory challenges, the first eight (or ten) persons constitute the jury.

F.   **Presentation of Evidence.** Please abide by the following rules:

- Do not enter the well, except during voir dire, opening statement and closing argument.
- Conduct all examination of witnesses from the podium.
- Feel free to approach witnesses during examination, but first seek permission from the Court. Please keep your visit to the witness stand brief, e.g., by quickly orienting the witness with an exhibit and returning to the podium.
- Where a party has more than one lawyer, only one lawyer may conduct the examination of a given witness and that lawyer alone may make objections concerning that witness.
- When objecting, state only the legal ground for the objection, e.g., "Objection, hearsay." Speaking objections are not permitted, unless the Court requests further information from counsel.
- Refrain from talking to each other in the presence of the jury. If clarification on a matter is needed, please seek clarification from the Court and not directly from counsel.
- Do not vouch for evidence, e.g., "I believe...."
- Refrain from facial expressions, nodding or other conduct that projects an opinion, favorable or unfavorable, concerning testimony of a witness, argument by counsel, or a ruling by the Court.
- Do not address or refer to witnesses or parties by first name alone, except for young witnesses under age 18. Use appropriate titles, e.g., Mr., Ms., Mrs., Agent, Officer, Doctor, etc.

G.   **Bench Conferences.** Sidebar conferences are disfavored. If counsel desire to speak to the Court outside the jury's presence, counsel may request to do so at the start of the recess or at the end of the day. Requests to see the Court outside the presence of the jury when the Court is about to begin the day of trial or reconvene following a recess generally will not be granted. These matters usually can await the next recess.

H.   **Exhibits.** Each counsel should submit a list of exhibits to the Courtroom Deputy Clerk on the first day of trial. All exhibits must be pre-marked on the first day of trial. Exhibit stickers may be obtained from the Courtroom Deputy Clerk or the intake window of the Clerk's Office, in advance of trial. Plaintiffs should mark their exhibits numerically and defendants by alphabetic letters. Civ. L.R. 16.1.f.2.c.

Counsel must show each other all exhibits, except for those intended to impeach witnesses which may be shown at sidebar and cleared by the Court immediately before the exhibit is intended to be used. When referring to an exhibit, counsel should refer to its exhibit number whenever possible to ensure a complete and accurate record.

Before publishing an exhibit to the jury, counsel either must move for admission of the exhibit or allow the Court to inquire whether the opposing side has any objection to publication.

Exhibits generally will be admitted at the close of all evidence.

Pursuant to Local Civil Rule 79.1, all exhibits will be returned to the moving party at the conclusion of the trial.

I. **Trial Schedule.**

(1) <u>Trial Days.</u> Generally, trials are scheduled from 9:00 a.m. to 4:30 p.m., beginning on Mondays. Trials do not proceed on Friday unless the jury is deliberating. Jury deliberations proceed from 9:00 a.m. to 4:30 p.m. The Court will notify the parties of deviations from this schedule and will attempt to accommodate jurors, witnesses and counsel, if conflicts arise.

(2) <u>Time Limits.</u> It is the practice of the Court to set a reasonable time limit for the entire trial. This time limit reflects the estimates of counsel but is based on the Court's independent assessment of the time necessary to complete the trial. Such a time limit is all-inclusive, and includes jury selection, opening statements, presentation of evidence, closing argument, and sidebar and jury instruction conferences. Time limits are subject to exception for good cause shown. The Courtroom Deputy Clerk will keep track of time and inform the parties periodically of the remaining time, generally at the end of each trial day.

(3) Witness Coordination. The Court attempts to accommodate witnesses' schedules and may permit counsel to call witnesses out of sequence if warranted by the circumstances. Counsel must anticipate any such possibility and discuss it with opposing counsel and the Court at the earliest possible time. At the end of each trial day, counsel will be invited to disclose the next day's witnesses to ensure orderly presentation of witnesses and adequate preparation for cross-examination.

9. **Courtesy.** Be courteous and respectful at all times, in all settings. Counsel may expect such from the Court, and the Court expects such from counsel. Please be familiar with and abide by Civil Local Rule 83.4.

B.   *Criminal Pretrial and Trial Procedures*

Criminal Pretrial and Trial Procedures of Judge Dana M. Sabraw

Unless otherwise ordered, matters before Judge Sabraw shall be conducted in accordance with the following practices:

1.   Communications with Chambers.

A.   Letters. Letters to chambers are prohibited, unless specifically requested by the Court. If letters are requested, copies of the same shall be simultaneously delivered to all counsel. Copies of correspondence between counsel shall not be sent to the Court.

B.   Faxes. Faxes to chambers are prohibited, unless specifically requested by the Court. If faxes are requested, copies of the same shall be simultaneously faxed or delivered to all counsel. Pleadings that are filed with the Clerk's Office may be faxed to chambers, provided that copies are simultaneously faxed or delivered to all counsel. Do not follow with a hard copy. The chambers fax number is 619-702-9942.

C.   Telephone Calls. Telephone calls to chambers are permitted. For matters other than docketing, scheduling or calendaring, call chambers at 619-557-6262, and address your inquiries to the Law Clerks. For docketing, scheduling and calendaring matters, call Courtroom Deputy Clerk Jamie Klosterman at 619-557-6399.

D.   Requests for Continuances. All requests for continuances should be made as soon as counsel become aware of the need for a continuance by contacting the Courtroom Deputy Clerk at the number above. If counsel stipulate to the requested continuance, a stipulation and order should be filed with chambers at the earliest practicable time and no later than 48 hours before the scheduled appearance. The stipulation and order should include the original date, the requested date for continuance, and the grounds for continuance.

2.   Motions.

A.   Scheduling a Hearing Date. The magistrate judge will set a date for pretrial motions. Any changes to that date or any other hearing date for motions shall be obtained from the Courtroom Deputy Clerk. Criminal Local Rule 47.1(a). Motions generally are heard on the Court's Friday calendar at 11:00 a.m.

B.   Filing of Motion Papers and Courtesy Copies. The original of all motions, including exhibits, on behalf of any defendant or any moving party, except the United States, shall be accompanied with two conformed copies and filed with the clerk at least 14 days before the date for which the motion is noticed unless the Court, for good cause and by order only, shortens such time. Criminal Local Rule 47.1(b).

C.   Notice to Court of Disposition. Any time a case is calendared for motions and counsel for either side knows that a disposition is to take place, counsel has a duty to call the Courtroom Deputy Clerk at the earliest available time to inform the Court of the disposition.

3.   Dispositions and Sentencings.

A.   Dispositions. Rule 11 guilty pleas may be taken by the magistrate judges on a report and recommendation. Because the magistrate judge may have a more flexible schedule, the Court encourages pleas before the magistrate judge assigned to the case. Rule 11 proceedings before the district judge may occur at the pretrial motion date or as scheduled by obtaining a date from the Courtroom Deputy Clerk.

B. Immediate Sentencing. Upon request, the Court will proceed with immediate sentencing in certain immigration cases if it has sufficient information in the record to perform a meaningful exercise of sentencing authority. Such dispositions are encouraged.

4. Trial Procedures.

A. Motions *in Limine*. At the pretrial motions date, the Court generally will schedule a hearing date for motions *in limine* at 11:00 a.m. on the Friday before the Monday trial call. Motions *in limine* are due two weeks before the hearing, with any opposition due one week before the hearing.

B. Jury Instructions. The parties should each submit proposed jury instructions to the Court on the first day of trial, unless otherwise ordered by the Court. Supplemental instructions must be filed and served as soon as the need for them becomes apparent. If counsel requests the model Ninth Circuit jury instructions, counsel may list the number of the instruction and edition without citing the text.

The Court prefers to use the Ninth Circuit Criminal Jury Instructions whenever possible. The Court will accept other proposed jury instructions but counsel must cite the authority supporting the proposed instructions. Any proposed modification of an instruction from statutory authority or the Ninth Circuit Models must state specifically the modification and the authority supporting the modification.

Before the case is submitted to the jury, the Court will provide each party with the jury instructions the Court intends to use. It is each party's responsibility to carefully review the instructions and make suggestions to the Court if modifications appear necessary.

C. Trial Briefs. Pursuant to Criminal Local Rule 23.1, the parties may, no later than five court days before the date of trial, serve and file briefs on all significant disputed issues of law, including foreseeable procedural and evidentiary issues.

D. Proposed *Voir Dire* Questions and Verdict Forms. Counsel may serve and file proposed *voir dire* questions and forms of verdict on the day set for motions *in limine*.

E. Jury Selection. The Courtroom Deputy Clerk will provide counsel with a numerical list of the jury panel at the start of *voir dire*, along with a seating chart. Jurors assigned seat numbers one through thirty-two will be questioned.

The number of jurors questioned (thirty-two) is calculated as follows: the number of jurors to be selected (twelve), the number of alternates to be selected (generally two), and the number of peremptory challenges (generally eighteen). Thus, in a single defendant case in which the defendant has ten and Government six peremptory challenges, plus one challenge each with respect to alternates, *voir dire* will result in thirty-two panelists.

The Court will conduct the initial jury *voir dire*. On a case by case basis, the Court may permit follow-up *voir dire* conducted by the attorneys. If *voir dire* by counsel is permitted, ten minutes per side on non-complex cases generally will be allowed.

After the Court and counsel have *voir dired* the panel, counsel may exercise challenges for cause outside the presence of the prospective jurors. If any challenges for cause are sustained, the removed panelists usually will be replaced by inserting new panelists from the *venire* so that a full panel exists before any peremptory challenges are exercised. The new panelists will be *voir dired* in accordance with the above.

The exercise of peremptory challenges will follow. Counsel will exercise alternating challenges – outside the presence of the prospective jurors – by calling out the jurors' numbers they wish to excuse. The process will be repeated until all peremptory challenges are exhausted.

In a single defendant case, the Government may exercise one challenge, followed by the defendant's exercise of two challenges for four rounds, then each side may exercise one challenge for two rounds, making a total of six and ten. These challenges may be exercised only as to panelists one through twenty-eight, that is, not as to the panelists from whom the alternates will be chosen.

Note that a party may waive its right to challenge but may not reserve. Thus, if counsel passes one time, he or she may not exercise any more peremptory challenges. Also note that challenges may be made to any of the panelists regardless of where that panelist appears in the array (except as to the prospective alternate jurors, that is, jurors twenty-nine through thirty-two). When each side has exhausted its peremptory challenges, the first twelve unchallenged persons shall constitute the jury.

After the twelve-person jury is selected, each side has one additional peremptory challenge which is exercisable only with respect to panelists twenty-nine through thirty-two, that is, the prospective alternates. Generally, two alternates are selected from the remaining unchallenged panelists. These final two challenges will occur after the peremptory challenges as to the initial twelve jurors have been exercised.

F. **Presentation of Evidence.** Please abide by the following rules:

- Do not enter the well, except during voir dire, opening statement and closing argument.
- Conduct all examination of witnesses from the podium.
- Feel free to approach witnesses during examination, but first seek permission from the Court. Please keep your visit to the witness stand brief, e.g., by quickly orienting a witness with an exhibit and returning to the podium.
- Where a party has more than one lawyer, only one lawyer may conduct the examination of a given witness and that lawyer alone may make objections concerning that witness.
- When objecting, state only the legal ground for the objection; e.g., "Objection, hearsay." Speaking objections are not permitted, unless the Court requests further information from counsel.
- Refrain from talking to each other in the presence of the jury. If clarification on a matter is needed, please seek clarification from the Court and not directly from counsel.

G. **Bench Conferences.** Sidebar conferences are disfavored. If counsel desire to speak to the Court outside the jury's presence, counsel may request to do so at the start of the recess or at the end of the day. Requests to see the Court outside the presence of the jury when the Court is about to begin the day of trial or reconvene following a recess generally will not be granted. These matters usually can await the next recess.

H. **Exhibits.** Government counsel must provide a list of exhibits and give it to the Courtroom Deputy Clerk on the first day of trial. All exhibits must be pre-marked on the first day of trial. Exhibit stickers may be obtained from the Clerk of the Court or from the Courtroom Deputy Clerk, in advance of the trial.

Before publishing an exhibit to the jury, counsel either must move for admission of the exhibit or allow the Court to inquire whether the opposing side has any objection to publication.

When referring to an exhibit, counsel should refer to its exhibit number whenever possible in order to keep a complete record.

If a demonstrative exhibit is being used and counsel's view is obstructed, counsel may relocate for better viewing without requesting permission from the Court.

Pursuant to Local Criminal Rule 1.1(e) and Local Civil Rule 79.1, all exhibits will be returned to the party who produced them at the conclusion of the trial.

I. **Trial Schedule.** Generally, trials are scheduled from 9:00 a.m. to 4:30 p.m., beginning on Mondays. Trials do not proceed on Friday unless a jury is deliberating. Jury deliberations proceed from 9:00 a.m. to 4:30 p.m. The Court will notify the parties of deviations from this schedule and will attempt to accommodate jurors, witnesses and counsel, if conflicts arise.

5. **Courtesy.** Be courteous and respectful at all times, in all settings. Counsel may expect such from the Court, and the Court expects such from counsel. Please be familiar with and abide by Civil Local Rule 83.4.

Hon. Janis L. Sammartino
District Judge

Chambers Information
U.S. District Court, Southern District of California
Courtroom 6, 3rd Floor
940 Front Street
San Diego, CA 92101

Scheduling Information
Courtroom Deputy: (619) 557-5291

Biographical Information
Born 1950 in Philadelphia, PA

Federal Judicial Service:
- Judge, U. S. District Court, Southern District of California
- Nominated by George W. Bush on March 19, 2007, to a seat vacated by Judith Nelsen Keep; Confirmed by the Senate on September 10, 2007, and received commission on September 21, 2007.

Education:
- Occidental College, A.B., 1972
- University of Notre Dame Law School, J.D., 1975

Professional Career:
- Law clerk, Hon. Douglas Seely, Superior Court, St. Joseph County, Indiana, 1975-1976
- Deputy city attorney, San Diego City Attorney's Office, California, 1976-1994
- Judge, Municipal Court of the City of San Diego, California, 1994-1995
- Judge, Superior Court of San Diego County, California, 1995-2007

Hon. Gordon Thompson, Jr.
District Judge

Chambers Information
U.S. District Court, Southern District of California
Courtroom 8, 3rd Floor
940 Front Street
San Diego, CA 92101

Scheduling Information
Courtroom Deputy: (619) 557-7486

Biographical Information
Born 1929 in San Diego, CA

Federal Judicial Service:
- Judge, U. S. District Court, Southern District of California
- Nominated by Richard M. Nixon on October 7, 1970, to a new seat created by 84 Stat. 294; Confirmed by the Senate on October 13, 1970, and received commission on October 16, 1970. Served as chief judge, 1984-1991. Assumed senior status on December 28, 1994.

Education:
- University of Southern California, B.S., 1951
- Southwestern University School of Law, LL.B., 1956

Professional Career:
- Deputy district attorney, County of San Diego, California, 1957-1960
- Private practice, San Diego, California, 1960-1970

Hon. Thomas J. Whelan
District Judge

Chambers Information
U.S. District Court, Southern District of California
Courtroom 7, 3rd Floor
940 Front Street
San Diego, CA 92101

Scheduling Information
Courtroom Deputy: (619) 557-6417

Criminal Law and Motion	Mondays at 2:00 p.m.

Biographical Information
Born 1940 in San Diego, CA

Federal Judicial Service:
- Judge, U. S. District Court, Southern District of California
- Nominated by William J. Clinton on June 4, 1998, to a seat vacated by John S. Rhoades; Confirmed by the Senate on October 21, 1998, and received commission on October 22, 1998.

Education:
- University of San Diego, B.A., 1961
- University of San Diego School of Law, J.D., 1965

Professional Career:
- Contracts administrator, planner, and estimator, General Dynamics Corp., 1961-1969
- Deputy district attorney, San Diego, CA, 1969-1989
- Judge, Superior Court of California, San Diego County, CA, 1990-1998

I. **Judge Whelan's Procedures and Practices**
   A. *Chambers Rules for Civil Cases*

CHAMBER RULES
The Honorable Thomas J. Whelan

These rules will help civil litigants appearing before Judge Whelan. They answer many commonly-received questions and explain procedures that are specific to Judge Whelan's chambers. In most cases, these rules are designed to help litigants clarify the issues and limit the scope of disputes before seeking the Court's assistance. The latest copy of these rules is available on the court's web site (http://www.casd.uscourts.gov).

Counsel for plaintiff, or plaintiff, if appearing on his or her own behalf, is responsible for promptly serving notice of the requirements contained herein upon defendant or defendant's counsel. If the action came to the Court via noticed removal, this burden falls on the removing defendant.

LOCAL RULES

Except as otherwise provided herein or as specifically order by the Court, all parties are expected to strictly comply with this District's Local Rules.

DISCOVERY

Pursuant to Civil Local Rules 26.1(e) and 72.1(b), discovery matters are handled by the assigned Magistrate Judge. All documents relating to discovery shall contain the words **"DISCOVERY MATTER"** in their caption to ensure proper routing. Hearings for discovery motions shall be scheduled by the assigned Magistrate Judge's law clerks.

MOTIONS
Hearing Dates

Counsel shall obtain all hearing dates from the Court's law clerks before filing moving papers. Any hearing dates for motions to be heard before Judge Whelan scheduled by the Magistrate Judge assigned to the case shall be cleared with Judge Whelan's law clerks before the parties file their moving papers.

Oral Argument

The Court generally decides motions based on the papers submitted by the parties. In the caption of its notice of motion and motion, the moving party shall include the following: **NO ORAL ARGUMENT PURSUANT TO LOCAL RULE.** If the Court decides that oral argument will assist it in deciding a given motion, counsel will be notified telephonically three court days before the scheduled hearing date.

Points and Authorities

In their memoranda of points and authorities, the parties shall state all legal and factual bases for their respective positions. Moving parties shall raise all factual and legal bases for the motion in the opening brief. Factual matters or legal arguments raised by a party for the first time in their reply brief, unless directly in response to the opposition, may not be considered.

Statement of Non-Opposition, Failure to Oppose

A party that determines that it will not oppose a given motion shall file a statement of non-opposition no later than 14 days before the hearing date. An opposing party's failure to file a memorandum of points and authorities in opposition to any motion will be construed as consent to the granting of the motion.

Reconsideration Motions

Motions for reconsideration are disfavored unless a party shows that there is new evidence, a change in controlling law, or establishes that the Court committed clear error in its earlier ruling. **No motion for reconsideration shall be filed without leave of the court.** No later than the time provided in Civil Local Rule 7.1(I)(2), the party seeking to move for reconsideration shall file an *ex parte* application for leave to file a motion to reconsider. The *ex parte* application shall be accompanied by a declaration as required by Civil Local Rule 7.1(I)(1). The application shall contain a brief summary of the argument the party intends to present in an motion for reconsideration, and shall not exceed **four pages in length**. Upon review of the application, the court will either issue an order granting leave to file a motion for reconsideration, including a briefing schedule, or an order denying leave. *Ex parte* applications made under this section shall be exempt from these rule's and the Local Rule's notice requirements.

Motions to Amend the Pleadings

Before filing any motions to amend the pleadings, counsel are required to meet and confer in good faith regarding the proposed amendment. To facilitate this process, the party seeking to amend their pleading shall provide opposing counsel with a copy of the proposed amended pleading along with an explanation of the reasons for the amendment. If counsel are unable to reach agreement regarding the proposed amendment, counsel filing the motion to amend shall attach a declaration to the motion to amend documenting counsels' meet and confer efforts.

All requests to amend the pleadings are handled by the Magistrate Judge assigned to the case. Please call the Magistrate Judge's law clerks to obtain a hearing date and submit all papers to the Magistrate Judge.

TEMPORARY RESTRAINING ORDERS

All motions for temporary restraining orders shall be briefed. While temporary restraining orders may be heard ex parte, the Court will do so only in extraordinary circumstances. The Court's strong preference is for the opposing party to be served and afforded a reasonable opportunity to file an opposition. In appropriate cases, the Court may issue a limited restraining order to preserve evidence pending further briefing. The Court will generally give notice of hearing by telephone.

ADMINISTRATIVE REQUESTS, *EX PARTE* APPLICATIONS

Before filing any *ex parte* application, counsel shall make every attempt to contact the opposing party to meet and confer regarding the subject of the *ex parte* application. All *ex parte* applications shall be accompanied by a declaration from counsel documenting (1) efforts to contact opposing counsel, (2) counsel's meet and confer efforts and (3) opposing counsel's position regarding the *ex parte* application. Any *ex parte* application filed with the Court shall be served on the opposing counsel via facsimile, electronic mail with return receipt requested or overnight mail. *Ex parte* applications that are not opposed within two Court days will be considered unopposed and may be granted on that ground.

CONTINUANCES

Parties requesting a continuance of any conference, hearing, deadline, briefing schedule, or other procedural changes, shall meet and confer prior to contacting the Court. If the parties reach an agreement, they shall submit a stipulation and proposed order with a detailed declaration of the reason for the requested continuance or extension of time. Except in extraordinary circumstances, stipulations to amend a briefing schedule or a motion hearing date must be filed no later than three court days before the affected date. If the parties are unable to reach an agreement, the party requesting the continuance shall file an *ex parte* application satisfying the applicable legal standard, with a particular focus on the diligence of the party seeking delay and any prejudice that may result therefrom. In addition, the *ex parte* application shall state (1) the original date, (2) the number of previous continuance requests and (3) whether previous requests were granted or denied.

FORMAT FOR PROPOSED ORDERS AND STIPULATIONS
Notice that order is "Proposed"

Please place the word "proposed" in brackets (e.g. "[PROPOSED] ORDER GRANTING EX PARTE APPLICATION TO..." "STIPULATION EXTENDING THE TIME IN WHICH TO FILE A RESPONSIVE PLEADING AND [PROPOSED] ORDER THEREON").

Extraneous Information Omitted

Remove any attorney or firm information from the headers, footers, or margins of the document. This includes attorney captions at the top left of the page, any firm logos in the left margin, document names in the bottom margin, etc.

Motions *in Limine*

Before filing any motions *in limine*, parties are required to meet and confer in an attempt to resolve their dispute. If the parties are unable to resolve their differences, counsel filing the motion *in limine* shall attach a declaration documenting the parties meet and confer efforts and the reason for their failure. Parties are encouraged to be selective with their motions *in limine* and not to file mundane or unnecessary motions.

Motions *in Limine* must be filed and served no later than **four weeks** before trial and any opposition must be filed no later than **two weeks** before trial. Reply papers should not be filed.

JURY INSTRUCTIONS

The parties are required to meet and discuss proposed jury instructions. If the parties are unable to reach an agreement, they may submit those instructions upon which they cannot agree to the Court.

COMMUNICATION WITH THE COURT

Consistent with Local Rule 83.9, counsel and parties shall refrain from writing letters or placing telephone calls to the Court or sending the Court copies of letters addressed to others, or otherwise causing or encouraging *ex parte* communications with the Court. Any party or attorney who causes or encourages such unauthorized *ex parte* communications or provides the Court's contact information with the knowledge that it shall be used for unauthorized *ex parte* communications, may be sanctioned. **Absent extraordinary circumstances, counsel shall personally initiate any authorized communications with the Court or chambers staff, rather than rely on a representative (*e.g.*, a secretary or**

paralegal).

PRE-TRIAL CONFERENCES/LETTER BRIEFS

In addition to submitting the Proposed Pretrial Order as required by the Civil Local Rules, the parties are further to separately submit informal letter briefs, not exceeding two single spaced pages, served on opposing counsel and received in Judge Whelan's chambers (and not filed in the Clerk's Office) no later than the **Wednesday before the pretrial conference at 2:30 p.m.**

The letter brief should be a relatively informal and straight forward document. The letter brief should outline a short, concise and objective factual summary of the party's case in chief, the number of hours/days each party intends to expend at trial, the approximate number of witnesses, whether certain witnesses will be coming in from out of town, the number of testifying expert witnesses, whether any unique demonstrative exhibits may be presented, the number of proposed motions *in limine* that may be filed, precisely when the parties would be prepared to submit their *in limine* papers (and whether the parties have met and conferred with respect to the *in limine* issues), the issue of proposed jury instructions and when the parties intend to submit them before trial, any *voir dire* issues, either party's preference as to what date(s) the trial should begin and any other pertinent information that either party may deem useful to assist the Court in the execution of the Pretrial Conference and in setting the matter for trial.

B.   *Chambers Rules for Criminal Cases*

1.   Communications with Chambers

   A.   **Letters.** Letters to chambers are prohibited, unless specifically requested by the Court. If letters are requested, copies of the same shall be simultaneously delivered to all counsel. Copies of correspondence between counsel shall not be sent to the Court.

   B.   **Faxes.** Faxes to chambers are prohibited, unless specifically requested by the Court. If faxes are requested, copies of the same shall be simultaneously faxed or delivered to all counsel. The chambers fax number is (619) 702-9915.

   C.   **Telephone Calls** For criminal matters, call the Courtroom Deputy, Bernadette Borja at 619-557-6417 or in the courtroom at 619 557-2677 (no voice mail at this number), for civil matters, call chambers at 557-6625.

   D.   **Requests for Continuances.** Judge Whelan does not continue criminal cases by joint motion or stipulation. Criminal cases are continued in open court. A party seeking a continuance of a hearing must notify the Courtroom Deputy at the earliest possible time.

2.   General Court Information

Criminal hearings, such as, sentencings, OSC's, dispositions and status hearings are scheduled on Monday's at 9:00 a.m. Motion hearings set by the Court are heard on Monday's at 2:00 p.m. A limited number of sentencings are also scheduled Tuesdays at 9:00 a.m.

3.   Pretrial Release

Pretrial Release decisions and modifications of release conditions are to be made by the Magistrate Judge, subject to appeal. A transcript shall be attached to any appeal to Judge Whelan of the Magistrate Judge's rulings regarding bail.

4.   Disposition Hearings

Judge Whelan prefers to handle dispositions in his cases. However, if he is not available, he does not object to counsel scheduling dispositions before the Magistrate Judges.

5.   Late Filing of Documents

When filing a document late, counsel shall submit a paper copy to chambers.

6.   TRIAL INFORMATION

Normal trial hours: Tuesdays through Thursdays: 9:00 a.m. to 12:00 noon & 1:00 p.m. To 4:00 p.m. Fridays: 9:00 a.m. to 1:00 p.m.

In Limine motions are heard the morning of trial prior to the jury impanelment.

Counsel are requested to pre-mark exhibits with plaintiff/government counsel using numbers and defense using letters.

Government counsel shall provide a list of exhibits to the courtroom deputy on the first day of trial.

Jury Selection: The courtroom deputy will provide counsel with a numerical list of the jury panel along with a seating chart. Judge Whelan seats 12 jurors and permits counsel to voir dire after the jurors have answered a short jury questionnaire. Counsel exercise their peremptory challenges in open court, on the record.

Jury Instructions: Judge Whelan prefers to use the Ninth Circuit Criminal Jury Instructions when possible.

Where a party has more than one lawyer, only one may object during direct or cross-examination of a given witness.

It is defense counsel's responsibility to arrange for an in custody, criminal defendant to be dressed in appropriate clothing ahead of time, consistent with the procedures at the institution where the defendant is being housed.

All trial exhibits are returned to counsel at the conclusion of trial.

If the defendant does not require an interpreter, it is counsel's responsibility to notify the clerk or interpreter section, in advance, of the need for an interpreter for a witness.

Counsel shall refrain from using foreign languages on the record in court. The Court Reporter only transcribes in English.

MAGISTRATE JUDGES

Hon. Jan M. Adler
Magistrate Judge

Chambers Information
U.S. District Court, Southern District of California
Courtroom A, 1st Floor
940 Front Street
San Diego, CA 92101

Scheduling Information
Courtroom Deputy: (619) 557-6412

Criminal Matters	Tuesdays and Thursdays at 2:00 p.m., unless otherwise scheduled by the Court.

Biographical Information
[Not available]

I.   **Judge Adler's Procedures and Practices**
A.   *Chambers Rules*

CHAMBERS RULES

Please Note: The Court provides this information for general guidance to counsel. However, the Court may vary these procedures as appropriate in any case.

Communications With Chambers
A. Letters, faxes, or emails. Letters, faxes, or emails to chambers are prohibited unless specifically requested by the Court. If letters, faxes, or emails are requested, copies of the same must be simultaneously delivered to all counsel. Copies of correspondence between counsel must not be sent to the Court.

B. Telephone Calls. Telephone calls to chambers are permitted only for matters such as scheduling and calendaring. Court personnel are prohibited from giving legal advice or discussing the merits of a case. Call the chambers at (619) 557-5585 and address your inquiries to the law clerk assigned to the case.

Early Neutral Evaluation ("ENE") Conference or Other Settlement Conferences
Counsel seeking to reschedule an ENE or other settlement conference must confer with opposing counsel prior to making the request. Such requests may be made by calling the law clerk assigned to the case at (619) 557-5585, and will be granted only upon good cause shown.

The Court requires all named parties, all counsel, and any other person(s) whose authority is required to negotiate and enter into settlement to appear **in person** at the ENE and other settlement conferences. Please see the order scheduling the conference for more information. The Court will **not** grant requests to excuse a required party from personally appearing absent extraordinary circumstances. Distance of travel alone does **not** constitute an "extraordinary circumstance." If counsel still wish to request that a required party be excused from personally appearing, they must confer with opposing counsel prior to making the request. Such requests may then be made by calling the law clerk at (619) 557-5585.

Case Management Conferences ("CMC")
The Court conducts the majority of its CMCs telephonically and, unless otherwise directed, initiates all conference calls. Counsel shall notify the law clerk of the telephone number at which they can be reached, if they will not be at their usual office number, in advance of the conference by calling the law clerk at (619) 557-5585. It is not necessary for counsel to contact chambers in advance of the conference call if he or she can be reached at their usual office number.

CMC statements are usually **not** required.

Case Management and Discovery Disputes
A. Counsel are to promptly meet and confer regarding all disputed issues, pursuant to the requirements of Civil Local Rules 16.5.k and 26.1.a. If counsel are in the same county, they are to meet in person; if counsel practice in different counties, they are to

confer by telephone. Under no circumstances may counsel satisfy the "meet and confer" obligation by written correspondence.

The Court expects strict compliance with the meet and confer requirement, as it is the experience of the Court that the vast majority of disputes can be resolved by means of that process. Counsel must **thoroughly** meet and confer and shall make every effort to resolve all disputes without the necessity of court intervention.

B. If the parties have not resolved their dispute through the meet and confer process, counsel shall, within **forty-five (45) days of the date upon which the event giving rise to the dispute occurred (see C. below)**, file a joint statement entitled "Joint Motion for Determination of Discovery Dispute" with the Court.

    1.   The joint statement is to include (1) A declaration of compliance with the meet and confer requirement and (2) Points and authorities (not to exceed 10 pages per side).[1]

    2.   Any exhibits accompanying the joint statement shall also be filed.

    3.   Counsel shall not attach copies of any meet and confer correspondence to the joint statement.

    4.   Please see Section 2.e of the Court's <u>Electronic Case Filing Administrative</u> Policies and Procedures Manual[2] to determine whether a courtesy copy of the joint statement needs to be delivered to chambers.

C. For oral discovery, the event giving rise to the discovery dispute is the completion of the transcript of the affected portion of the deposition. For written discovery, the event giving rise to the discovery dispute is the service of the response.

D. The Court will either issue an order following the filing of the joint statement or will schedule a telephonic discovery conference.

Stipulated Protective Order Provisions for Filing Documents Under Seal

All stipulated protective orders submitted to the Court need to include the following provisions:

> Subject to public policy, and further court order, nothing shall be filed under seal, and the Court shall not be required to take any action, without separate prior order by the Judge before whom the hearing or proceeding will take place, after application by the affected party with appropriate notice to opposing counsel.
>
> If the Court grants a party permission to file an item under seal, a duplicate disclosing all nonconfidential information, if any, shall be filed and made part of the public record. The item may be redacted to eliminate confidential material from the document. The document shall be titled to show that it corresponds to an item filed under seal, e.g., "Redacted Copy

---

[1]   The Court expects counsel to be succinct and to the point in all written submissions. It is the Court's philosophy that brevity is the soul of wit.

[2]   This Manual can be found online at the Court's website www.casd.uscourts.gov.

of Sealed Declaration of John Smith in Support of Motion for Summary Judgment." The sealed and redacted documents shall be filed simultaneously.

All stipulated protective orders submitted to the Court must be filed as a joint motion, and must include a proposed order. Please refer to Sections 2.f.4 and 2.h of the Court's <u>Electronic Case Filing Administrative Policies and Procedures Manual</u> for more information.

General Decorum

The Court expects all counsel and parties to be courteous, professional, and civil at all times to opposing counsel and parties, and the Court, including all court personnel. Professionalism and civility -- in court appearances, communications with chambers, and written submissions – are of paramount importance to the Court. Personal attacks on counsel or opposing parties will not be tolerated under any circumstances.

Technical Questions Relating to CM/ECF

If you have a technical question relating to CM/ECF, please contact the CM/ECF Help Desk at (866) 233-7983.

Inquiries Regarding Criminal Matters

All inquiries regarding criminal matters shall be directed to Judge Adler's courtroom deputy, Rhea Rhone, at (619) 557-6412.

B.   *Criminal Pretrial Procedures*

CRIMINAL PRETRIAL PROCEDURES

Please Note: The Court provides this information for general guidance to counsel. However, the Court may vary these procedures as appropriate in any case.

CRIMINAL CALENDAR:

Judge Adlers' Courtroom Deputy ("CRD"), Rhea Rhone, handles all criminal inquiries on criminal matters. Her telephone number is (619) 557-6412.

Criminal calendars are heard on Tuesdays and Thursdays at 2:00p.m., unless otherwise scheduled by the Court. Criminal Arraignments will be held during duty week at 10:30a.m. And 2:00p.m. as scheduled by the Court. For Tuesday and Thursday calendars, counsel shall check in with the Court's CRD no later than 1:45pm. Counsel are expected to be punctual and to advise the Court's CRD of any scheduling conflicts in advance of their hearing.

PRESENTMENT OF BAIL DOCUMENTS:

The bail documents, in the format approved by the Court, shall be presented to the Judge's Courtroom Deputy for review prior to being accepted in chambers. The bail documents must include a copy of the Order of Conditions of Release as applicable to the defendant in the case.

Material witness bonds must include a notation in the upper right hand corner of the arraignment date of the material witness.

BAIL MODIFICATION HEARINGS:

Bail Modifications will not be heard unless calendared in advance and with at least 24 hours notice to the opposing party, Pretrial Services, and the sureties.

NEBBIA HEARINGS:

Nebbia hearings will only be held if calendared in advance with no less than 24 hours notice to all parties and the assigned Pretrial Services officer. Defense counsel must provide the Court and the United States Attorney's Office a copy of the proposed bail package, including appraisals, title documents, and other relevant materials at least 24 hours in advance of the hearing.

ARRAIGNMENT ON INFORMATIONS:

Counsel shall have the written Waiver of Indictment signed by their client prior to the scheduled hearing.

CHANGE OF PLEA:

Changes of plea will only be heard if calendared in advance. Counsel shall have the written consent to Rule 11 Plea form signed by their client prior to the scheduled hearing.

MISDEMEANOR SENTENCINGS:

Counsel shall file a sentencing summary chart and/or sentencing memorandum no later than two (2) days before the sentencing hearing or change of plea hearing (if requesting immediate sentencing).

Hon. Ruben B. Brooks
Magistrate Judge

Chambers Information
U.S. District Court, Southern District of California
Courtroom B, 1st Floor
940 Front Street
San Diego, CA 92101

Scheduling Information
Courtroom Deputy: (619) 557-7143

Biographical Information
[Not available]

Hon. Mitchell D. Dembin
Magistrate Judge

Chambers Information

U.S. District Court, Southern District of California
Courtroom E, 1st Floor
940 Front Street
San Diego, CA 92101

Scheduling Information

Courtroom Deputy: (619) 557-5973

Criminal Matters	Tuesdays and Thursdays at 1:30 p.m., unless otherwise scheduled by the Court.

Biographical Information

[Not available]

I.   Judge Dembin's Procedures and Practices
A.   *Chambers Rules – Civil Pretrial Procedures*

CHAMBERS RULES
CIVIL PRETRIAL PROCEDURES

Please note: The Court provides this information for general guidance to counsel. However, the Court may vary these procedures as appropriate in any case.

Local Rules

Except as otherwise provided herein or as specifically ordered by the Court, all parties are expected to strictly comply with the Local Rules of the United States District Court for Southern District of California.

Communications with Chambers

A. **Letters, Faxes and Emails.** Letters, faxes and emails to chambers are discouraged unless specifically requested by the Court. If letters, faxes, or emails are requested, copies of the same must be simultaneously delivered to all counsel. Copies of correspondence between counsel should not be sent to the Court.

B. **Telephone Calls.** With the exception of scheduled telephonic conferences, telephone calls to chambers are permitted only for matters such as scheduling and calendaring. Court personnel are prohibited from giving legal advice or discussing the merits of a case. Call the chambers at (619) 446-3972 and address your inquiries to the law clerk assigned to the case.

Early Neutral Evaluation ("ENE") Conference and other Settlement Conferences

Counsel seeking to reschedule an ENE or other settlement conference must confer with opposing counsel prior to making the request. After conferring with opposing counsel, such requests may be initiated by calling the law clerk assigned to the case at (619) 446-3972 as soon as counsel is aware of the good cause necessitating the request to continue but, absent compelling circumstances, must be made at least five (5) days prior to the scheduled conference. Following telephonic contact with chambers, counsel will be required to file an *ex parte* or Joint Motion, as appropriate, which will be granted only upon good cause shown.

The Court requires all named parties, all counsel, and any other person(s) whose authority is required to negotiate and enter into settlement to appear **in person** at the ENE and other settlement conferences. Please see the order scheduling the conference for more information. The Court will **not** grant requests to excuse a required party from personally appearing absent extraordinary circumstances. Distance of travel alone does **not** constitute an "extraordinary circumstance." Counsel requesting that a required party be excused from personally appearing must confer with opposing counsel prior to making the request. Such requests may then be made by calling the law clerk at (619) 446-3972.

A confidential ENE conference statement may be lodged with chambers no later than three (3) days before the ENE either by messenger or by email to the Court at efile_dembin@casd.uscourts.gov. Parties choosing to submit confidential ENE statements must include the following:

1. A brief description of the case and the claims asserted;

2. A specific and current demand for settlement addressing all relief or remedies sought. If a specific demand for settlement cannot be made at the time the brief is submitted, then the reasons therefore must be stated along with a statement as to when the party will be in a position to state a demand; and,

3. A brief description of any previous settlement negotiations, mediation sessions or mediation efforts.

If the case is settled in its entirety before the scheduled date of the ENE or settlement conference, counsel must file a Notice of Settlement or call chambers at (619) 446 3972 as soon as possible before the scheduled ENE or settlement conference.

Case Management

A. **Case Management Conferences ("CMC").** The Court conducts the majority of its CMCs telephonically, and unless otherwise directed, Plaintiff's counsel coordinates and initiates all conference calls.

B. **Discovery Plans.** The parties are required to submit a **Joint Discovery Plan** at least one week before the scheduled CMC. The plan must be one document and must explicitly and in detail address each item identified in Fed.R.Civ.P. 26(f)(3). In addition, the discovery plan must specifically address:

   i. Whether there is limited discovery that may enable each party to make a reasonable settlement evaluation such as the deposition of plaintiff, defendant, or key witnesses, and the exchange of a few pertinent documents;

   ii. The need for discovery of electronically stored information, any issues regarding production of such information and the form or forms in which it should be produced;

   iii. Whether there are issues in the case requiring expert evidence, including whether counsel anticipates any issues under *Daubert v. Merrell Dow Pharm., Inc.*, 509 U.S. 579 (1993);

   iv. The procedure the parties plan to use regarding claims of privilege; and,

   v. Whether a protective order will be needed in the case.

C. **Requests to Amend the Schedule.** The dates and times set in the Scheduling Order **will not** be modified except for good cause shown. Fed.R.Civ.P. 16(b)(4). Counsel are reminded that they must "take all steps necessary to bring an action to readiness for trial." Civil Local Rule 16.1(b). Any requests for extensions must be made by filing a Joint Motion. The motion shall include a declaration from counsel of record detailing the steps taken to comply with the dates and deadlines set in the order, and the specific reasons why deadlines cannot be met.

Discovery Disputes

A. **Meet and Confer Requirements:** Counsel must meet and confer on all issues before contacting the court. If counsel are located in the same district, the meet and confer must be in person. If counsel are located in different districts, then telephone or video conference may be used. In no event will meet and confer letters, facsimiles or emails satisfy this requirement.

B. **Depositions:** If a dispute arises during the course of a deposition regarding an issue of privilege, enforcement of a court-ordered limitation on evidence, or pursuant to Fed.R.Civ.P. 30(d), counsel are to meet and confer prior to seeking any ruling from the Court. If the matter is not resolved prior to seeking a ruling, counsel may call chambers at 619-446-3972 and seek a ruling. If the Court is unable to review the matter at that moment, counsel are to proceed with he deposition in other areas of inquiry and the court will respond as soon as practicable. If the matter cannot readily be resolved by the Court, the Court may require the parties to file a Motion as provided at subparagraph C below.

C. **Disputes Over Written Discovery Requests:** If the dispute concerns written discovery requests (e.g. interrogatories, requests for production) or an oral discovery dispute that could not be resolved in a telephonic conference with the Court, the parties shall submit a **"Joint Motion for Determination of Discovery Dispute."** The Joint Motion is to include the following:

1. The exact wording of the document or things requested to be produced or the exact wording of the interrogatory or request for admission asked;

2. The exact response to the request by the responding party;

3. A statement by the propounding party as to why a further response should be compelled; and,

4. A precise statement by the responding party as to the basis for all objections and/or claims of privilege.

The joint motion shall be accompanied by: (1) a declaration of compliance with the meet and confer requirement; and, (2) points and authorities (not to exceed five (5) pages per side). **Copies of meet and confer correspondence shall not be attached to the joint motion.**

D. **Timing of Motions:** Any motion related to discovery disputes, including motions to compel discovery and motions for a protective order relative to discovery shall be brought by joint motion as described in Section C above and must be filed no later than thirty (30) days after the date upon which the event giving rise to the dispute occurred. For oral discovery, the event giving rise to the dispute is the completion of the transcript of the affected portion of the deposition. For written discovery, the event giving rise to the discovery dispute is the service of the response, **not** the date on which counsel reach an impasse in meet and confer efforts.

Ex-Parte Proceedings

The Court does not have regular *ex parte* hearing days or hours. Appropriate *ex parte* applications which, as a general rule, does not include discovery disputes, may be made at any time after first contacting the law clerks, but must ultimately be filed electronically on ECF and include a description of the dispute, the relief sought, and accompanied by a separate affidavit indicating reasonable and appropriate notice to the opposition. After service of the *ex parte* application, opposing counsel will ordinarily be given until 5:00 p.m. on the next business day to respond. If more time is needed, opposing counsel must call the law clerk assigned to their case to modify the schedule. After receipt, moving and opposing *ex parte* papers will be reviewed and a decision will be made without a hearing. If the Court requires a hearing, the parties will be contacted to set a date and time.

Stipulated Protective Orders

Any protective order submitted for the Court's signature must contain the following two provisions:

(1) No document shall be filed under seal unless counsel secures a court order allowing the filing of a document under seal. An application to file a document under seal shall be served on opposing counsel, and on the person or entity that has custody and control of the document, if different from opposing counsel. If opposing counsel, or the person or entity who has custody and control of the document, wishes to oppose the application, he/she must contact the chambers of the judge who will rule on the application, to notify the judge's staff that an opposition to the application will be filed.

(2) The Court may modify the protective order for good cause, in the interests of justice or for public policy reasons on its own initiative.

In addition, it is recommended that the stipulated protective order contain a provision regarding the disposition of confidential or sealed documents and information after the case is closed.

All stipulated protective orders shall be filed as a joint motion. The parties shall email directly to chambers a proposed order, in Word or WordPerfect format, containing the text of the protective order.

Procedure for Filing Documents Under Seal

There is a presumptive right of public access to court records based upon common law and First Amendment grounds. Accordingly, no document may be filed under seal, i.e., closed to inspection by the public, except pursuant to a Court order that authorizes the sealing of the particular document, or portions thereof. A sealing order may issue only upon a request that establishes that the document, or portions thereof, is privileged or otherwise subject to protection under the law. The request must be narrowly tailored to seek sealing only of sensitive personal or confidential information. Upon the granting of an application to file a document under seal, a redacted version shall be e-filed. A physical copy of the unredacted version must be lodged with chambers.

General Decorum

The Court expects all counsel and parties to be courteous, professional, and civil at all times to opposing counsel, parties, and the Court, including all court personnel. The importance of professionalism and civility in the proper functioning of the judicial system. It should go without saying that personal attacks on counsel or opposing parties will not be tolerated. Counsel are expected to be punctual for all proceedings and are reminded to follow Civil Local Rule 83.4, in their practice before this Court.

Technical Questions Relating to CM/ECF

If you have a technical question relating to CM/ECF, please contact the CM/ECF Help Desk at (866) 233-7983.

Inquiries Regarding Criminal Matters

All inquiries regarding criminal matters shall be directed to Judge Dembin's Courtroom Deputy at (619) 557-5973.

B. *Chambers Rules – Criminal Pretrial Procedures*

CHAMBERS RULES
CRIMINAL PRETRIAL PROCEDURES

Please note: The Court provides this information for general guidance to counsel. However, the Court may vary these procedures as appropriate in any case.

Local Rules

Except as otherwise provided herein or as specifically ordered by the Court, all parties are expected to strictly comply with the Local Rules of the United States District Court for Southern District of California.

Criminal Calendar

Criminal calendars are heard on Tuesdays and Thursdays at 1:30 PM, unless otherwise scheduled by the Court. Check the calendar for the location of the courtroom. Counsel are expected to be punctual. The Court expects counsel to have obtained their client's signature on all essential documents necessary for the hearing to proceed, including waivers of indictment, plea agreements and consent forms, in advance of the hearing. In cases in which the defendant will be sentenced by Judge Dembin, the Court requests that all sentencing documents be filed 24 hours in advance of the sentencing hearing.

Bail Modification Hearings

Absent extraordinary circumstances, bail modifications will not be heard unless calendared in advance and with 24 hours notice to the opposing party, the Pretrial Services Office, and the sureties. Parties must provide all documents being relied upon to Judge Dembin's Courtroom Deputy, as soon as practicable in advance of the hearing, preferably 24 hours in advance.

Bail Stipulations (Joint Motions) for Change of Bond Conditions

The Court will accept written joint motions for modification of bail conditions. The Joint Motion must be signed by all counsel, the defendant, the bond sureties, and the Pretrial Services Officer supervising the defendant, if any. A copy of the Order of Conditions of Release must be attached to the Joint Motion.

Presentation of Bail Documents

Bail documents, in the format approved by the Court, must be presented to Judge Dembin's Courtroom Deputy for review. The bail documents must include a copy of the Order of Conditions of Release applicable to the defendant. Material witness bonds must also be presented to the Courtroom Deputy and must include a notation, in the upper right hand corner of the bond, of the arraignment date of the material witness.

Nebbia Hearings

Nebbia hearings will only be heard if calendared in advance with no less than 24 hours notice to all parties and the Pretrial Services Office. Defense counsel must provide the Court and the United States Attorney's Office a copy of the proposed bail package, including appraisals, title documents, and other relevant materials, at least 24 hours in advance of the hearing.

Inquiries Regarding Criminal Matters

All inquiries regarding criminal matters shall be directed to Judge Dembin's Courtroom Deputy at (619) 557-5973.

Hon. William V. Gallo
Magistrate Judge

Chambers Information
U.S. District Court, Southern District of California
Courtroom F, 1st Floor
940 Front Street
San Diego, CA 92101

Scheduling Information
Courtroom Deputy: (619) 557-7141

Criminal Matters	Tuesdays and Thursdays at 2:00 p.m., unless otherwise scheduled by the Court.

Biographical Information
[Not available]

I.   **Judge Gallo's Procedures and Practices**
          A.   *Chambers Rules for Civil Cases*

CHAMBERS RULES

Please Note: The Court provides this information for general guidance to counsel. However, the Court may vary these procedures as appropriate in any case.

I.   **Communications With Chambers**

A.   **Letters, faxes, or emails.** Letters, faxes, or e-mails to chambers are disfavored unless specifically requested by the Court. If letters, faxes, or emails are requested, copies of the same must be simultaneously delivered to all counsel. Copies of correspondence between counsel should not be sent to the Court.

B.   **Telephone Calls.** Telephone calls to chambers are permitted only for matters such as scheduling and calendaring. Court personnel are prohibited from giving legal advice or discussing the merits of a case. Call Judge Gallo's chambers at (619) 557-6384 and address your scheduling inquiries to the Research Attorney assigned to the case.

C.   **Lodging Documents.** When an order directs you to "lodge" documents with the Court, either send it via e-mail to efile_Gallo@casd.uscourts.gov, or deliver the document to Judge Gallo's chambers.

II .   **Early Neutral Evaluation ("ENE") Conferences or Other Settlement Conferences ("SC")**

At least **five (5) court days prior to the ENE or SC**, the parties shall submit directly to Judge Gallo's chambers a ENE or SC Statement of **five (5)** pages or less, which outlines the nature of the case, the claims, the defenses, and the parties' positions regarding settlement of the case. The Statement may be submitted confidentially within the parties' discretion.

The ENE or SC statements may be mailed to Judge Gallo's chambers or e-mailed to: efile_Gallo@casd.uscourts.gov.

Statements in excess of **five (5)** pages will not be considered.

The Court generally allots two (2) hours for ENEs and SCs. Counsel should be prepared to be succinct and to the point. Requests for additional time must be made in writing and included in the party's ENE or SC Statement, accompanied by a short explanation.

The Court requires all named parties, all counsel, and any other person(s) whose authority is required to negotiate and enter into settlement to appear **in person** at the ENE and other Scs. Please see the order scheduling the conference for more information. The Court will not grant requests to excuse a required party from personally appearing, absent extraordinary circumstances. Distance or cost of travel alone does not constitute an "extraordinary circumstance." If counsel still wish to request that a required party be excused from personally appearing, they must confer with opposing counsel prior to making the request. Such requests may then be made by submitting the request in writing to Judge Gallo's chambers at least seven (7) days before the scheduled ENE or SC . The request may be mailed to Judge Gallo's chambers or e-mailed to: efile_Gallo@casd.uscourts.gov.

If the case is settled in its entirety before the scheduled date of the ENE or SC, counsel must file a Notice of Settlement or call Judge Gallo's chambers at (619)557-6384 as soon as possible, but no later than 24 hours before the scheduled ENE or SC.

III. **Case Management Conferences ("CMC")**

A. Ordinarily, the Court conducts its CMC's telephonically. Counsel must, and the parties may, participate in the CMC by telephone. Unless otherwise directed, the Court will initiate all conference calls. Prior to a telephonic CMC, counsel shall notify the Research Attorney assigned to the case of the telephone number at which they can be reached, **only** if they will **not** be at their usual office number. Counsel (and the parties) may request to appear in person subject to the approval of the Court. If personal appearance is requested, counsel must file a Joint Statement one (1) week before the scheduled CMC.

B. **Discovery Plans.** The parties are required to submit a **Joint Discovery Plan** one week before the scheduled CMC. The Joint Discovery Plan must be one document and must explicitly cover the parties' views and proposals for each item identified in Fed.R.Civ.P. 26(f)(3).

In addition, Judge Gallo requires the discovery plan to identify:

1. By name and/or title, all witnesses that counsel plans to depose in the case and a brief explanation as to why counsel wants to depose the witness. If counsel do not agree to the deposition of a specific witness, counsel must explain the legal basis for the objection;

2. Specific documents or categories of documents that counsel wants produced during discovery. If counsel disagree about the production of documents or categories of documents, the plan must articulate a specific and valid legal basis for the objection;

3. What limited discovery may enable them to make a reasonable settlement evaluation. e.g. deposition of plaintiff, defendant, or key witness, and exchange of a few pertinent documents;

4. What issues in the case implicate expert evidence, including whether counsel anticipates any issues under *Daubert v. Merrell Dow Pharm., Inc.*, 509 U.S. 579 (1993);

5. Threshold legal issues that may be resolved by summary judgment or partial summary judgment;

6. The procedure the parties plan to use regarding claims of privilege; and

7. Whether a protective order will be needed in the case.

8. A proposed schedule for:
   a. the filing of motions to amend pleadings and/or add parties;
   b. the completion of fact and expert witness discovery;

    c.   the designation and supplemental designation of expert witnesses;

    d.   the service of expert witness reports and rebuttal expert witness reports;

    e.   the date by which all motions, including dispositive motions, shall be filed;

    f.   a date for a Settlement Conference; and

    g.   a date for a Pretrial Conference before the District Judge assigned to the case.

Requests to Amend the Case Management Conference Order. The dates and times set in the Case Management Conference Order **will not** be modified except for good cause shown. Fed.R.Civ.P. 16(b)(4). Counsel are reminded of their duty of diligence and that they must "take all steps necessary to bring an action to readiness for trial." Civil Local Rule 16.1(b). Any requests for extensions must be made by filing a Joint Motion. The Joint Motion shall include a declaration from counsel of record detailing the steps taken to comply with the dates and deadlines set in the order, and the specific reasons why deadlines cannot be met.

IV.   <u>Discovery Disputes</u>

    A.   The Court will not accept motions pursuant to Federal Rules of Civil Procedure16, 26 through 37 and 45 until counsel have met and conferred to resolve the dispute and participated in an informal teleconference with the Court. Strict compliance with these procedures is mandatory before the Court will accept any discovery motions.

    B.   Counsel are to promptly meet and confer regarding all disputed issues, pursuant to the requirements of Civil Local Rule 26.1.a. If counsel are in the same county, they **shall** meet in person; if counsel practice in different counties, they **shall** confer by telephone. Under no circumstances may counsel satisfy the "meet and confer" obligation by written correspondence. Counsel must proceed with due diligence in scheduling and conducting an appropriate meet and confer conference as soon as the dispute arises.

        The Court expects strict compliance with the meet and confer requirement, as it is the experience of the Court that the vast majority of disputes can be resolved by means of that process. Counsel must **thoroughly** meet and confer and shall make every effort in good faith to resolve all disputes without the necessity of court intervention.

    C.   Counsel must participate in the Court's **informal dispute resolution procedure:** Counsel will call the Court to schedule a telephonic discovery conference. The Court may request counsel to submit a letter brief, not to exceed two (2) pages, that explains the discovery dispute, the parties' positions, and the reasons relief should be granted or denied.

    D.   If the dispute can not be resolved during the teleconference with the Court, counsel shall, within **thirty (30)** days of the date upon which the event giving rise to the dispute occurred (see F. below), e-file a Joint Statement with the Court entitled "Joint Statement For Determination Of Discovery Dispute." The Joint Statement shall include:

1. A declaration of compliance with the meet and confer requirement. Counsel **should not** attach copies of any meet and confer correspondence to the declaration or Joint Statement;

2. A specific identification of each dispute;

3. A joint statement of the dispute(s) must follow this format (see sample in subsection H. below):

    a. The exact wording of the discovery request in dispute;
    b. The exact objection of the responding party;
    c. A statement by the propounding party as to why the discovery is needed, including any legal basis to support the position;

4. The legal basis for the objection by the responding party.

5. **Without leave of Court, the joint motion, including exhibits, may not exceed ten (10) pages.**

6. Please see Section 2.e of the Court's Electronic Case Filing Administrative Policies and Procedures Manual[1] to determine whether a courtesy copy of the joint statement needs to be delivered to chambers.

E. If the dispute arises during a deposition, counsel may call Judge Gallo's chambers at (619) 557-6384 for an immediate ruling on the dispute. If Judge Gallo is available, he will either rule on the dispute or give counsel further instructions regarding how to proceed. If Judge Gallo is unavailable, counsel shall mark the deposition at the point of the dispute and continue with the deposition. Thereafter, counsel shall meet and confer regarding all disputed issues pursuant to the requirements of Civil Local Rule 26.1.a. If counsel have not resolved their disputes through the meet and confer process, they shall proceed as noted in paragraphs B and/or C above.

F. For oral discovery, the event giving rise to the discovery dispute is the completion of the transcript of the affected portion of the deposition. For written discovery, the event giving rise to the discovery dispute is the date of the service of the response.

G. The Court will either issue an order following the filing of the Joint Statement, schedule another telephonic discovery conference, or hold a hearing.

H. **Sample Format: Joint Statement for Determination Of Discovery Dispute**

    Request No. 1: Any and all documents referencing, describing or approving the Metropolitan Correctional Center as a treatment facility

---

[1] This Manual can be found online at the Court's website www.casd.uscourts.gov.

for inmate mental health treatment by the Nassau County local mental health director or other government official or agency.

Response to Request No. 1: Objection. This request is overly broad, irrelevant, burdensome, vague and ambiguous and not limited in scope as to time.

Plaintiff's Reason to Compel Production: This request is directly relevant to the denial of Equal Protection for male inmates. Two women's jails have specifically qualified Psychiatric Units with certain license to give high quality care to specific inmates with mental deficiencies. Each women's psychiatric Unit has specialized professional psychiatric treatment staff (i.e., 24 hour psychiatric nurses full time, psychiatric care, psychological care, etc.). Men do not have comparable services. This request will document the discrepancy. (Include relevant Points and Authorities.)

Defendant's Basis for Objections: This request is not relevant to the issues in the case. Plaintiff does not have a cause of action relating to the disparate psychiatric treatment of male and female inmates. Rather, the issue in this case is limited to the specific care that Plaintiff received. Should the Court find that the request is relevant, defendant request that it be limited to a specific time frame. (Include relevant Points and Authorities.)

V.   Stipulated Protective Order Provisions for Filing Documents Under Seal

All stipulated protective orders submitted to the Court must include the following provision:

No document shall be filed under seal unless counsel secures a court order allowing the filing of a document under seal. An application to file a document under seal shall be served on opposing counsel, and on the person or entity that has custody and control of the document, if different from opposing counsel. If opposing counsel, or the person or entity who has custody and control of the document, wishes to oppose the application, he/she must contact the chambers of the judge who will rule on the application, to notify the judge's staff that an opposition to the application will be filed.

If an application to file a document under seal is granted by Judge Gallo, a redacted version of the document shall be e-filed. A courtesy copy of the unredacted document shall be delivered to Judge Gallo's chambers.

All stipulated protective orders submitted to the Court must be filed as a Joint Motion, and must include a proposed order. Please refer to Sections 2.f.4 and 2.h of the Court's Electronic Case Filing Administrative Policies and Procedures Manual for more information.

VI.   *Ex Parte* Proceedings

Appropriate ex parte applications may be made at any time after first contacting Judge

Gallo's Research Attorney assigned to the case. The application must be e-filed and should include a description of the dispute, the relief sought, and a declaration that indicates reasonable and appropriate notice to opposing counsel, in accordance with Civil Local Rule 83.3.h. The Court does not have regular ex parte hearing days or hours.

After service of the ex parte application, opposing counsel will ordinarily be given until 5:00 PM on the next business day to respond. If more time is needed, opposing counsel must call Judge Gallo's Research Attorney assigned to the case to modify the schedule. After receipt of the application and opposition, the Court will review them and a decision may be made without a hearing. If the Court requires a hearing, the parties will be contacted to set a date and time for the hearing.

VII.   Requests to Continue

Whether made by Joint Statement or by *ex parte* application, any request to continue an Early Neutral Evaluation Conference, Settlement Conference, Case Management Conference, or Case Management Conference Order deadline shall be made in writing no less than **seven (7) calendar days** before the affected date. The request shall state:

1. The original date or deadline;

2. The number of previous requests for continuance;

3. A showing of good cause for the request;

4. Whether the request is opposed and why; and

5. Whether the requested continuance will affect other dates in the Case Management Conference Order.

Joint Motions For Continuance shall be made in the form required by Civil Local Rule 7.2.

VIII.   General Decorum

The Court expects all counsel and parties to be courteous, professional, and civil at all times to opposing counsel, parties, and the Court, including all court personnel. Counsel may expect such from the Court and the Court expects such from counsel. Professionalism and civility – in court appearances, communications with chambers, and written submissions -- are of paramount importance to the Court. Personal attacks on counsel or opposing parties will not be tolerated under any circumstances.

Counsel are to read and be familiar with the tenets espoused in Civil Local Rule 83.4, which shall be the guiding principles of conduct in this Court.

Counsel are expected to be punctual for all proceedings.

IX.   Technical Questions Relating to CM/ECF

If you have a technical question relating to CM/ECF, please contact the CM/ECF Help Desk at (866) 233-7983.

X.   Inquiries Regarding Criminal Matters

All inquiries regarding criminal matters shall be directed to Judge Gallo's Courtroom Deputy, Jennifer Yahl, at (619) 557-7141. Please see Judge Gallo's Criminal Pretrial Procedures.

B. *Criminal Pretrial Procedures*

CRIMINAL PRETRIAL PROCEDURES

Please Note: The Court provides this information for general guidance to counsel. However, the Court may vary these procedures as appropriate in any case.

CRIMINAL CALENDAR
Criminal calendars are heard on Tuesdays and Thursdays at 2:00 PM, unless otherwise scheduled by the Court. Counsel are expected to be punctual.

COURT DOCUMENTS
In an effort to expedite the proceedings, all documents requiring a client's signature should be signed, if at all possible, prior to the scheduled appearance in court, such as, but not limited to:
- Waivers of Indictment
- Plea Agreements
- Rule 11 Consent forms
- Consent to be tried by United States Magistrate Judge
- Rule 5 & 5.1 forms

BAIL MODIFICATION HEARINGS
Absent extraordinary circumstances, bail modifications will not be heard unless calendared in advance and with 24 hours notice to the opposing party, the Pretrial Services Office, and the sureties.

BAIL STIPULATIONS FOR CHANGE OF CONDITIONS
The Court will accept written stipulations for modification of bail conditions. Stipulations must be signed by all counsel, the defendant, the bond sureties, and the Pretrial Services Officer supervising the defendant, if any. A copy of the Order of Conditions of Release must be attached to the written stipulation.

PRESENTATION OF BAIL DOCUMENTS
Bail documents, in the format approved by the Court, must be presented to Judge Gallo's Courtroom Deputy for review, prior to being accepted in chambers. The bail documents must include a copy of the Order of Conditions of Release applicable to the defendant in the case.

Material witness bonds must include a notation, in the upper right hand corner of the bond, of the arraignment date of the material witness.

NEBBIA HEARINGS
Nebbia hearings will only be heard if calendared in advance with no less than 24 hours notice to all parties and the Pretrial Services Office. Defense counsel must provide the Court and the United States Attorney's Office a copy of the proposed bail package, including appraisals, title documents, and other relevant materials, 24 hours in advance of the hearing.

MISDEMEANOR SENTENCINGS

Counsel shall file a sentencing summary chart and/or sentencing memorandum no later than two (2) days before the sentencing hearing or change of plea hearing (if requesting immediate sentencing).

Hon. Peter C. Lewis
Magistrate Judge

Chambers Information
U.S. District Court, Southern District of California
2003 W. Adams Ave, Suite 220
El Centro, CA 92243

Scheduling Information
Courtroom Deputy: (760) 335-3429

Biographical Information
[Not available]

Hon. Barbara Lynn Major
Magistrate Judge

Chambers Information
U.S. District Court, Southern District of California
Courtroom H, 1st Floor
940 Front Street
San Diego, CA 92101

Scheduling Information
Courtroom Deputy: (619) 557-7099

Biographical Information
[Not available]

Hon. William McCurine, Jr.
Magistrate Judge

Chambers Information
U.S. District Court, Southern District of California
Courtroom C, 1st Floor
940 Front Street
San Diego, CA 92101

Scheduling Information
Courtroom Deputy: (619) 557-6425

Criminal Matters	Tuesdays and Thursdays at 9:30 a.m., unless otherwise scheduled by the Court.

Biographical Information
[Not available]

I.   Judge McCurine's Procedures and Practices
A.   *Chambers Rules – Civil Pretrial Procedures*

CHAMBER RULES
CIVIL PRETRIAL PROCEDURES

Please note: The Court provides this information for general guidance to counsel. However, the Court may vary these procedures as appropriate in any case.

Local Rules

Except as otherwise provided herein or as specifically ordered by the Court, all parties are expected to strictly comply with the Local Rules of the United States District Court for Southern District of California.

Communications with Chambers

A.   Letters. Letters to chambers are prohibited unless specifically requested by the Court. If letters are requested, copies of the same shall be simultaneously delivered to all counsel. Copies of correspondence between counsel shall not be sent to the Court.

B.   Faxes. Faxes to chambers are prohibited unless specifically requested by the Court. If faxes are requested, copies of the same shall be simultaneously delivered to all counsel.

C.   Telephone Calls. Telephone calls to chambers are permitted only for matters such as scheduling and calendaring. Court personnel are prohibited from giving legal advice or discussing the merits of a case. Call the chambers at 619-557-6624 and address your inquiries to the law clerk assigned to your case.

Early Neutral Evaluation (ENE)

The Southern District of California requires litigants in civil cases to meet with the assigned Magistrate Judge supervising discovery for an Early Neutral Evaluation Conference within forty-five days of filing an answer.[1]

In order to conduct the most effective ENE conference, each counsel must appear in person with a representative who has authority to discuss and enter into settlement. Judge McCurine and the parties will discuss the claims and defenses, and attempt to settle the case. The ENE conference is informal, off the record, privileged, and confidential.

A confidential ENE conference statement shall be lodged with chambers no later than seven (7) days before the ENE either by messenger or to the Court's email address at efile_mccurine@casd.uscourts.gov.

The ENE statements must include the following:

1.   A brief description of the case and the claims asserted;

2.   A specific and current demand for settlement addressing all relief or remedies sought. If a specific demand for settlement cannot be made at the time the brief is submitted, then the reasons therefore must be stated along

---

[1]   At the discretion of the Court, ENE and Case Management Conferences need not be set in the following categories of cases: (1) *habeas corpus* cases; (2) cases reviewing administrative rulings; (3) social security cases; (4) default proceedings; (5) cases in which a substantial number of defendants have not answered; (6) actions to enforce judgments; (7) bankruptcy appeals; and (8) section 1983 prisoner cases. Civil Rule 16.1.e.

with a statement as to when the party will be in a position to state a demand; and

3.   A brief description of any previous settlement negotiations, mediation sessions or mediation efforts.

Absent extraordinary circumstances, a request to continue the ENE will not be considered unless submitted via a motion to continue the date no less than fourteen (14) days prior to the scheduled conference.

If the case is settled in its entirety before the scheduled date of the conference, counsel must file a Notice of Settlement twenty-four (24) hours before the ENE conference.

If the case does not settle at the ENE conference, Judge McCurine may refer the case to mediation or arbitration.

If no settlement is reached at the ENE conference, a Case Management Conference ("CMC") will be held within 30 days after the ENE conference.

Case Management Conference (CMC)

The parties are required to lodge a Joint Discovery Plan under Rule 26 of the FRCP pursuant to court order either by messenger or to the Court's email address at efile_mccurine@casd.uscourts.gov.

The statement must include an estimate of the number of depositions, all discoverable documents, or other discovery that may be necessary for the judge to assess the needs of the case.

The Joint Discovery Plan, usually initiated by the plaintiff, must be one document. If the parties do not agree on the terms, each party can list their objections.

Procedures for the CMC are set forth in Civil Local Rule 16.1.d.

Mandatory Settlement Conference (MSC)

After the Case Management Conference, Judge McCurine will set a pre-trial schedule and a Mandatory Settlement Conference.

If the case does not settle at the MSC, the case will be handled by the assigned District Court Judge and proceed to trial.

Discovery Disputes

Judge McCurine requires the parties to attempt to resolve any discovery disputes by telephone or in-person. The Court will not accept motions pursuant to Rules 26 through 37 of the Federal Rules of Civil Procedure until counsel have: (1) previously met and conferred concerning all disputed issues; and (2) participated in a teleconference with the Court. See Civil Local Rule 26.1(a).

If the parties have not resolved their dispute through the meet and confer process, counsel shall contact the law clerk assigned to their case and provide a neutral statement of the dispute. The law clerk will then schedule a telephonic conference with both parties to resolve the dispute before Judge McCurine.

Ex-Parte Proceedings

Judge McCurine does not have regular *ex parte* hearing days or hours. Appropriate *ex parte* applications may be made at any time after first contacting the law clerks, but must ultimately be filed electronically on ECF and include a description of the dispute, the relief sought, and accompanied by a separate affidavit indicating reasonable and appropriate notice to the opposition.

After service of the *ex parte* application, opposing counsel will ordinarily be given until 5:00 p.m. on the next business day to respond. If more time is needed, opposing counsel must call the law clerk assigned to their case to modify the schedule. After receipt, moving and opposing *ex parte* papers will be reviewed and a decision will be made without a hearing. If the Court requires a hearing, the parties will be contacted to set a date and time.

General Decorum

All persons, whether observers, witnesses, lawyers, or clients, must maintain proper decorum while in Court.

Pursuant to Civil Local Rule 83.4, an attorney in practice before this Court shall:

(a)   Be courteous and civil in all communications, oral and written, and in all proceedings conduct herself/himself with dignity and respect.

(b)   Be a vigorous and zealous advocate on behalf of a client without acting in a manner detrimental to the proper functioning of the judicial system.

(c)   Attempt to resolve litigation consistent with his or her client's interests.

(d)   Attempt to informally resolve disputes with opposing counsel.

(e)   Agree to reasonable scheduling changes, requests for extensions of time and waivers of procedural formalities, if the legitimate interests of a client will not be adversely affected.

(f)   Communicate with opposing counsel in an attempt to establish a discovery plan and voluntary exchange of non-privileged information.

(g)   When possible, confer with opposing counsel before scheduling or rescheduling hearings, depositions, and meetings and notify all parties and the court, as early as possible, when hearings or depositions must be canceled.

B. *Chambers Rules – Criminal Pretrial Procedures*

CHAMBER RULES
CRIMINAL PRETRIAL PROCEDURES

Please note: The Court provides this information for general guidance to counsel. However, the Court may vary these procedures as appropriate in any case.

Local Rules

Except as otherwise provided herein or as specifically ordered by the Court, all parties are expected to strictly comply with the Local Rules of the United States District Court for Southern District of California.

Criminal Calendar

Criminal calendars are heard on Tuesdays and Thursdays at 9:30 a.m., unless otherwise scheduled by the Court. Criminal Arraignments will be held at 10:30 a.m. and 2:00 p.m. as scheduled by the Court.

Bail Modification Hearings

Bail modifications will not be heard unless calendared in advance and with 24-hour notice to the opposing party, Pretrial Services, and the sureties.

Bail Stipulations for Change of Conditions

The Court will accept written stipulations for modification of conditions as a general matter. Stipulations must be signed by all counsel, defendant, the bond sureties and the Pretrial Services Officer, if any, supervising the defendant. A copy of the Order of Conditions of Release must be attached.

Presentment of Bail Documents

Bail documents, in the format approved by the Court, should be presented to the Judge's Courtroom Deputy for review prior to be accepted in chambers. The bail documents must include a copy of the Order of Conditions of Release as applicable to the defendant in the case.

Nebbia Hearings

Nebbia hearings will only be heard if calendared in advance with no less than 24-hour notice to all parties and the Pretrial Services office. Defense counsel must provide the Court and the United States Attorney's Office a copy of the proposed bail package, including appraisals, title documents, and other relevant materials twenty-four (24) hours in advance of the hearing.

Arraignment on Informations

Counsel shall have the written Waiver of Indictment signed by their client prior to the scheduled hearing.

General Decorum

All persons, whether observers, witnesses, lawyers, or clients, must maintain proper decorum while in Court.

Hon. Louisa S. Porter
Magistrate Judge

Chambers Information
U.S. District Court, Southern District of California
Courtroom H, 1st Floor
940 Front Street
San Diego, CA 92101

Scheduling Information
Courtroom Deputy: (619) 557-6695

Biographical Information
[Not available]

I.   Judge Porter's Procedures and Practices
A.   *Civil Discovery Conferences*

CIVIL DISCOVERY CONFERENCES

DISCOVERY DISPUTE:

In an effort to save time and expense for all litigants, this Court holds discovery dispute conferences in lieu of formal noticed motions.

Should a discovery dispute arise during the course of the litigation in this case, the following procedure is to be followed:

> If a dispute arises during deposition, you are to call the Court for an immediate ruling. If the Court is unable to handle the matter at that moment, you are to proceed with the deposition and the Court will get back to you as soon as possible.

> For all other discovery disputes, you are to meet and confer regarding all disputed issues before contacting the Court. If all attorneys are local, you are required to meet and confer in person. If one or all attorneys are out of town, you are to meet and confer by phone. Under no circumstances will the meet and confer requirement be satisfied by written correspondence.

After you have met and conferred, you may contact the Court for a discovery conference date. The court will not consider any discovery matter unless, and until, a declaration of compliance with the meet and confer requirement is received.

In addition to a date for a discovery conference, you will also receive a date by which you are to submit a joint discovery conference statement and memorandum of points and authorities to the Court. The joint statement is to include the following:

1.   The exact wording of the document or things requested to be produced or the exact wording of the interrogatory or request for admission asked.

2.   The exact response to the request by the responding party.

3.   A statement by the propounding party as to why the documents should be produced or why the interrogatory or request for admission should be answered.

4.   A precise statement by the responding party as to the basis for all objections and/or claims of privilege, including the legal basis for all privileges.

The points and authorities:

1.   shall not exceed 10 pages per side.

2.   be submitted with joint discovery conference statement.

** Points and authorities exceeding 10 pages without prior approval will not be considered by the Court.

SAMPLE: JOINT DISCOVERY CONFERENCE STATEMENT

REQUEST NUMBER 1:

Any and all documents referencing, describing or approving the Metropolitan Correctional Center as a treatment facility for inmate mental health treatment by the Nassau County local mental health director or other government official or agency.

RESPONSE TO REQUEST NUMBER 1:

Objection. This request is overly broad, irrelevant, burdensome, vague and ambiguous and not limited in scope as to time.

PLAINTIFF'S REASON WHY DOCUMENTS SHOULD BE PROVIDED:

This request is directly relevant to the denial of Equal Protection for male inmates. Two women's jails have specifically qualified Psychiatric Units with certain license to give high quality care to specific inmates with mental deficiencies. Each women's psychiatric Unit has specialized professional psychiatric treatment staff (i.e., 24 hour psychiatric nurses full time, psychiatric care, psychological care, etc.). Men do not have comparable services. This request will document the discrepancy.

DEFENDANT'S BASIS FOR OBJECTIONS:

This request is not relevant to the issues in the case. Plaintiff does not have a cause of action relating to the disparate psychiatric treatment of male and female inmates. Rather, the issue in this case is limited to the specific care that Plaintiff received.

Should the Court find that the request is relevant, defendant request that it be limited to a specific time frame.

B. *Protective Orders*

PROTECTIVE ORDERS

All Protective Orders shall include language addressing the following:

(1) What the Court shall do with confidential or sealed documents after the case is closed (i.e., how the documents are to be disposed). The language should indicate whether the documents are to be destroyed or returned to the parties and the time frame in which to do either. Further, the Protective Order must state that any action by this Court must be preceded by an ex parte motion for an order authorizing the return of all Confidential and Attorneys' Eyes Only Material to the party that produced the information or the destruction thereof.

(2) The manner in which documents are to be filed under seal. If a party wishes to file document(s) under seal, they may not rely solely upon the Protective Order. Rather, the party must seek leave of court to file the particular document(s) under seal from the judge presiding over the particular hearing for which they wish to file the document(s). The Clerk's office will not automatically file document(s) under seal without a court order corresponding to the particular document(s).

(3) Modification of the Protective Order by the Court. The Protective Order shall state that the Court may modify the terms and conditions of the Order for good cause, or in the interest of justice, or on its own order at any time in these proceedings.

(4) Relation to any court or local rules. The Protective Order shall state that without separate court order, the Protective Order and the parties' stipulation does not change, amend, or circumvent any court rule or local rule.

Hon. Bernard G. Skomal
Magistrate Judge

Chambers Information
U.S. District Court, Southern District of California
Courtroom H, 1st Floor
940 Front Street
San Diego, CA 92101

Scheduling Information
Courtroom Deputy: (619) 557-7104

Criminal Matters	Tuesdays and Thursdays at 2:00 p.m.

Biographical Information
[Not available]

I.   **Judge Skomal's Procedures and Practices**
A.   *Chambers Rules*

CHAMBERS RULES

Please Note: The Court provides this information for general guidance to counsel. However, the Court may vary these procedures as appropriate in any case.

Communications With Chambers

A. Code of Conduct. Counsel are directed to review and be familiar with Civil Local Rule 83.4. This Court will hold counsel to the standards set forth in the rule and will enforce the standards through sanctions or disciplinary action as provided in Civil Local Rules 83.1 and 83.5.

B. Letters, faxes, or emails. Letters, faxes, or emails to chambers are not permitted unless specifically requested by the Court. If letters, faxes, or emails are requested, copies of the same must be simultaneously delivered to all counsel. Copies of correspondence between counsel should not be sent to the Court. Unauthorized correspondence will be rejected.

C. Telephone Calls. Telephone calls to chambers are permitted only for matters such as calendaring or addressing discovery disputes. Court personnel are prohibited from giving legal advice or discussing the merits of a case on an ex parte basis. Call Judge Skomal's chambers at (619) 557-2993 and address your inquiries to the Research Attorney assigned to the case. When calling chambers, be prepared to identify your case number.

D. Conference Calls. When an order, minute order, or other notice from the Court directs you to "coordinate and initiate the conference call," the initiating party should make arrangements for all call participants to be on the phone and then should call chambers at the time set for the call. The Court cannot advise you on how to coordinate the conference or a particular conferencing service to use.

E. Lodging Documents. When an order directs you to "lodge" documents with chambers (usually your ENE and MSC statements), you should either send it via email to: efile_Skomal@casd.uscourts.gov, or deliver the document directly to chambers.

Courtesy Copies

Courtesy copies of filings exceeding 20 pages shall be delivered directly to chambers, 101 W. Broadway, Suite 1100. Unless expressly required by the Court, courtesy copies must be identical to the electronically-filed documents. The pages of each pleading must be firmly bound and must be 2-hole punched at the top. If a pleading has more than three (3) exhibits, the exhibits must be tabbed.

Early Neutral Evaluation ("ENE") Conference or Other Settlement Conferences

At least five (5) court days prior to the ENE, the parties shall submit directly to Judge Skomal's chambers a confidential ENE Statement of five (5) pages or less, which outlines the nature of the case, the claims, the defenses, and the parties' positions regarding settlement of the case.

The settlement position must include a specific and current demand or offer addressing all relief or remedies sought. If a specific demand or offer cannot be made at the time the brief is submitted, then the reasons therefor must be stated along with a statement as to when the party will be in a position to state a demand or offer. General statements that a party will "negotiate in good faith" is not a specific demand or offer.

The ENE statements may be hand delivered to Judge Skomal's chambers or e-mailed to: **efile_Skomal@casd.uscourts.gov.**

Counsel seeking to reschedule an ENE or other settlement conference must confer with opposing counsel **prior** to making the request. Such requests may be made by filing a joint motion or an ex parte application and will be granted by Judge Skomal only upon good cause shown. At the time the request is filed, a proposed Order must also be submitted in Word or WordPerfect format to efile_Skomal@casd.uscourts.gov. Such requests should be made as soon as counsel is aware of the good cause warranting rescheduling the conference, but in no event should be made less than one week prior to the scheduled conference.

The Court requires all named parties, all counsel, and any other person(s) whose authority is required to negotiate and enter into settlement to appear in person at the ENE and other settlement conferences. Please see the order scheduling the conference for more information. The Court will **not** grant requests to excuse a required party from personally appearing, absent extraordinary circumstances. Distance of travel alone does not constitute an "extraordinary circumstance." If counsel still wish to request that a required party be excused from personally appearing, they must confer with opposing counsel prior to making the request. Such requests may then be made by filing a joint motion or an ex parte application. At the time the request is filed, a proposed Order must also be submitted in Word or WordPerfect format to efile_Skomal@casd.uscourts.gov.

If the case is settled in its entirety before the scheduled date of the ENE or settlement conference, counsel must file a Notice of Settlement and call Judge Skomal's chambers at (619)557-2993 as soon as possible before the scheduled ENE or settlement conference.

Case Management

A. **Case Management Conferences ("CMC").** The Court conducts the majority of its CMCs telephonically, and unless otherwise directed, Plaintiff's counsel coordinates and initiates all conference calls.

B. **Discovery Plans.** The parties are required to file a **Joint Discovery Plan** at least one week before the scheduled CMC. The plan must be one document and must explicitly cover the parties views and proposals for **each** item identified in Fed.R.Civ.P. 26(f)(3). In addition, Judge Skomal requires the discovery plan to identify whether the parties will consent to jurisdiction of a Magistrate Judge. Agreements made in the Discovery Plan will be treated as binding stipulations that are effectively incorporated into the Court's Case Management Order.

In cases involving significant document production and electronic discovery, the parties must also include the process and procedure for "claw back" or "quick peek" agreements as contemplated by Fed. R. Evid. 502(d). The parties should also address whether an order providing for protection under Rule 502(e) is needed.

C. **Requests to Amend the Schedule.** The dates and times set in the Scheduling Order **will not** be modified except for good cause shown. Fed.R.Civ.P. 16(b)(4). Counsel are reminded of their duty of diligence and that they must "take all steps necessary to bring an action to readiness for trial." Civil Local Rule 16.1(b).

Any requests for extensions should be made by filing a Joint Motion. The motion shall include a declaration from counsel of record detailing the steps taken to comply with the dates and deadlines set in the order, and the specific reasons why deadlines cannot be met. A party seeking a modification may move ex parte if the other parties will not join in a motion to amend the schedule. The declaration must address the steps counsel took to obtain a stipulation. When the motion is made after time has expired, Fed. R. Civ. P. 6(b)(1)(B) requires the parties to address excusable neglect.

Discovery Responsibilities

The Parties are to strictly comply with the provisions of Fed. R. Civ. P. 26(g)(1-2). Failure to comply, without substantial justification, will result in sanctions as mandated by Rule 26(g)(3).

Discovery Disputes

1. **The Court will not accept any discovery motion that does not strictly comply with the following procedures.**

2. Counsel are to promptly meet and confer regarding all disputed issues. If counsel are located in the same district, you are _required_ to meet and confer in person. If counsel are located in different districts, you are to meet and confer by phone or video conference. Counsel must proceed with due diligence in scheduling and conducting an appropriate meet and confer conference as soon as a dispute arises. If a party is unresponsive to a request to meet and confer, after 48 hours contact chambers and the Court will issue an order setting a telephonic conference with the research attorney assigned to the case.

3. If the dispute arises during a deposition regarding an issue of privilege, enforcement of a court ordered limitation on evidence, or pursuant to Fed.R.Civ.P. 30(d), counsel should suspend the deposition and immediately meet and confer. If the dispute is not resolved after meeting and conferring, counsel may call Judge Skomal's chambers at (619) 557-2993 for an immediate ruling on the dispute. If Judge Skomal is available, he will either rule on the dispute or give counsel further instructions on how to proceed. If Judge Skomal is unavailable, counsel must mark the deposition at the point of the dispute and continue with the deposition. Thereafter, counsel shall meet and confer regarding all disputed issues pursuant to the requirements of Civil Local Rules 16.5.k. and 26.1.a. If counsel have not resolved their disputes through the meet and confer process, they shall proceed as noted in paragraph 4 below.

4. If the parties have not resolved the dispute through the meet and confer process,

counsel for all interested parties must promptly and **jointly** contact Judge Skomal's chambers and speak with the research attorney assigned to the case. Counsel must be prepared to specifically and succinctly explain the dispute to the research attorney. Counsel must agree on the issue(s) in dispute prior to calling chambers. The research attorney will explain the issue to Judge Skomal. The Court will either set a telephonic discovery conference or advise the parties to file a motion. Counsel are again reminded that they must abide by the Court's rules regarding conduct and proper decorum during calls with the research attorney.

Under no circumstance will Judge Skomal rule on a discovery dispute that is brought to his attention more than thirty (30) days after the date upon which the event giving rise to the dispute occurred absent good cause (see paragraph 7 below). If the discovery dispute may result in the need to amend the schedule, the parties will also be required to comply with the procedure for extending the schedule as set forth above.

5. If Judge Skomal requests that the parties file a discovery motion, the Court will advise the parties of the format for the motion.

6. For oral discovery, the event giving rise to the discovery dispute is the completion of the transcript of the affected portion of the deposition. For written discovery, the event giving rise to the discovery dispute is service of the response or the time for such service if no response is given.

7. Counsel should not stop conducting other discovery due to a dispute.

Protective Order Provisions

All stipulated protective orders submitted to the Court must include the following provisions:

1. What the Court shall do with confidential or sealed documents after the case is closed (i.e.,how the documents are to be disposed). The language should indicate whether the documents are to be destroyed or returned to the parties and the time frame in which to do either. Further, the Protective Order must state that any action by this Court must be preceded by an ex parte motion for an order authorizing the return of all Confidential and Attorneys' Eyes Only Material to the party that produced the information or the destruction thereof.

2. Modification of the Protective Order by the Court. The Protective Order shall state that the Court may modify the terms and conditions of the Order for good cause, or in the interest of justice, or on its own order at any time in these proceedings.

3. Relation to any court or local rules. The Protective Order shall state that without separate court order, the Protective Order and the parties' stipulation does not change, amend, or circumvent any court rule or local rule.

4. Filing documents under Seal. The Protective Order must include the language: No document shall be filed under seal unless counsel secures a court order allowing the filing of a document under seal. An application to file a document under seal shall be served on opposing counsel, and on the person or entity that has custody and control of the document, if different from opposing counsel. If

opposing counsel, or the person or entity who has custody and control of the document, wishes to oppose the application, he/she must contact the chambers of the judge who will rule on the application, to notify the judge's staff that an opposition to the application will be filed.

If an application to file a document under seal is granted by Judge Skomal, a redacted version of the document shall be e-filed. A courtesy copy of the unredacted document shall be delivered to Judge Skomal's chambers.

All stipulated protective orders submitted to the Court must be filed as a Joint Motion, and must include a proposed order. Please refer to Sections 2.f.4 and 2.h of the Court's Electronic Case Filing Administrative Policies and Procedures Manual for more information.

General Decorum

The Court expects all counsel and parties to be courteous, professional, and civil at all times to opposing counsel, parties, and the Court, including all court personnel. Professionalism and civility—in court appearances, communications with chambers, and written submissions—are of paramount importance to the Court. Personal attacks on counsel, parties, or court staff will not be tolerated under any circumstance. Inappropriate behavior will be subject to sanctions as provided in Civ. Local Rules 83.1 and 83.5.

Technical Questions Relating to CM/ECF

If you have a technical question relating to CM/ECF, please contact the CM/ECF Help Desk at (866) 233-7983.

Inquiries Regarding Criminal Matters

All inquiries regarding criminal matters shall be directed to Judge Skomal's Courtroom Deputy, Trish Lopez, at (619) 557-7104.

B. *Criminal Pretrial Procedures*

CRIMINAL PRETRIAL PROCEDURES

Please Note: The Court provides this information for general guidance to counsel. However, the Court may vary these procedures as appropriate in any case.

CRIMINAL CALENDAR

Criminal calendars are heard on Tuesdays and Thursdays at 2:00 PM, unless otherwise scheduled by the Court. Counsel are expected to be punctual.

BAIL MODIFICATION HEARINGS

Absent extraordinary circumstances, bail modifications will not be heard unless calendared in advance and with 24 hours notice to the opposing party, the Pretrial Services Office, and the sureties. Parties must provide all documents being relied upon to Judge Skomal's Courtroom Deputy, Trish Lopez, preferably 24 hours in advance of the hearing, or as soon as practicable in advance of the hearing.

BAIL STIPULATIONS FOR CHANGE OF CONDITIONS

The Court will accept written stipulations for modification of bail conditions. Stipulations must be signed by all counsel, the defendant, the bond sureties, and the Pretrial Services Officer supervising the defendant, if any. A copy of the Order of Conditions of Release must be attached to the written stipulation.

PRESENTATION OF BAIL DOCUMENTS

Bail documents, in the format approved by the Court, must be presented to Judge Skomal's Courtroom Deputy for review. The bail documents must include a copy of the Order of Conditions of Release applicable to the defendant in the case.

Material witness bonds must include a notation, in the upper right hand corner of the bond, of the arraignment date of the material witness. Material witness bonds must also be presented to Judge Skomal's Courtroom Deputy for review.

NEBBIA HEARINGS

Nebbia hearings will only be heard if calendared in advance with no less than 24 hours notice to all parties and the Pretrial Services Office. Defense counsel must provide the Court and the United States Attorney's Office a copy of the proposed bail package, including appraisals, title documents, and other relevant materials, 24 hours in advance of the hearing.

Hon. Nita L. Stormes

Presiding Magistrate Judge

Chambers Information

U.S. District Court, Southern District of California
Courtroom G, 1st Floor
940 Front Street
San Diego, CA 92101

Scheduling Information

Courtroom Deputy: (619) 557-7749

Biographical Information

[Not available]

I.   Judge Stormes' Procedures and Practices
A.   Civil Case Procedures

CIVIL CASE PROCEDURES

Please Note: The Court provides this information for general guidance to counsel. However, the Court may vary these procedures as appropriate in any case.

Communications with Chambers

Chambers staff includes two law clerks and one courtroom deputy. The law clerks handle inquiries on civil matters while the courtroom deputy handles inquiries on criminal matters. The telephone number for the law clerks is (619) 557-5391. The telephone number for the courtroom deputy is (619) 557-7749.

A. Letters, faxes, or emails. Letters, faxes or emails to chambers are prohibited except for as set forth in these guidelines.

B. Lodging Documents. When an order directs you to "lodge" documents with chambers (usually, your ENE brief, MSC statement or discovery plan), you should bring the document directly to chambers (e.g., via an attorney courier service). If the total number of pages, including exhibits, is 20 or less, you may lodge the document via email at efile_stormes@casd.uscourts.gov.

C. Telephone Calls. Telephone calls to chambers are permitted only for procedural matters such as scheduling a conference or motion with the Court. The Court's law clerks are not permitted to give legal advice, nor are they allowed to discuss how or when the court will rule on a disputed matter. Law clerks will not discuss complex procedural issues with anyone other than counsel for the parties.

Ex Parte Proceedings

The Court does not have regular *ex parte* days or hours, and discovery disputes are not generally resolved via *ex parte* application. Appropriate ex parte applications must be filed electronically on CM/ECF and include a description of the dispute, the relief sought, reasonable and appropriate notice to the opposition and an attempt to resolve the dispute without the court's intervention. After service of the ex parte application, opposing counsel will ordinarily be given until 5:00 p.m. the next business day to respond. If more time is needed, opposing counsel must call the court's law clerk at (619) 557-5391 to modify the schedule. After receipt of the application and opposition the Court will issue a decision without a hearing.

Continuances

Whether made by joint motion or *ex parte* application, any request to continue an Early Neutral Evaluation conference, settlement conference or scheduling order deadline shall be made in writing no less than **seven (7) calendar days** before the affected date. The request shall state:

1.   The original deadline or date;

2.   The number of previous requests for continuance;

3.   A showing of good cause for the request;

4. Whether the request is opposed and why; and

5. Whether the requested continuance will affect other case management dates.

Joint motions for continuance shall be in the form required by **Local Rule 7.2.**

Early Neutral Evaluation ("ENE") Conference or other Settlement Conferences

No later than **three (3) court days** before the ENE, the parties shall **lodge confidential statements** of five pages or less directly with the chambers of Magistrate Judge Stormes outlining the nature of the claims and defenses and their settlement position.

The court requires all named parties, all counsel, and any other person(s) [e.g. insurance adjusters] whose authority is required to negotiate and enter into a full and binding settlement to appear **in person** at the ENE and other settlement conferences. A **government entity** is excused from this requirement so long as the government attorney who attends the ENE conference has (1) primary responsibility for handling the case; and (2) authority to negotiate and recommend settlement offers to the government official(s) having ultimate settlement authority.

The Court will **not** grant requests to excuse a required party from personally appearing absent "extraordinary circumstances." Distance of travel or expense alone do not constitute "extraordinary circumstances."

Case Management Conferences (CMCs)

The Court conducts the majority of its CMCs by telephone, unless otherwise directed.

Discovery Disputes

A. Timing of Motions: Any motion to compel discovery or a motion for a protective order relative to discovery shall be brought by joint motion as described in Section "D" below and filed no later than 45 days after the date upon which the event giving rise to the dispute occurred. For oral discovery, the event giving rise to the dispute is the completion of the transcript of the affected portion of the deposition. For written discovery, the event giving rise to the discovery dispute is the service of the response, **not** the date on which counsel reach an impasse in meet and confer efforts.

B. Meet and Confer Requirements: Counsel must meet and confer on all issues **before** contacting the court. If counsel are located in the same district, the meet and confer must be in person. If counsel are located in different districts, then telephone or video conference may be used. In no event will meet and confer letters, facsimiles or emails satisfy this requirement.

C. Depositions: If a dispute arises during the course of a deposition, you are to call the Court's law clerks and ask the court for a ruling. If the Court is unable to review the matter at that moment, you are to proceed with the deposition in other areas of inquiry and the court will get back to you.

D. Disputes Over Written Discovery Requests: If the dispute concerns written discovery requests (e.g. interrogatories, requests for production), the parties shall submit a **"Joint Motion for Determination of Discovery Dispute."** The Joint Motion is to include:

1.   The exact wording of the document or things requested to be produced or the exact wording of the interrogatory or request for admission asked;

2.   The exact response to the request by the responding party;

3.   A statement by the propounding party as to why a further response should be compelled; and

4.   A precise statement by the responding party as to the basis for all objections and/or claims of privilege.

Any such joint motion shall be accompanied by (1) a declaration from **lead** trial counsel of compliance with the meet and confer requirement and (2) points and authorities (not to exceed 10 pages per side). **Counsel shall not attach copies of their meet and confer correspondence to the joint motion.** See sample format attached to Scheduling Order Regulating Discovery.

Stipulated Protective Orders

Any protective order submitted for the Court's signature must contain these **two** provisions:

> Nothing shall be filed under seal, and the court shall not be required to take any action, without separate prior order by the Judge before whom the hearing or proceeding will take place, after application by the affected party with appropriate notice to opposing counsel. The parties shall follow and abide by applicable law, including Civ. L.R. 79.2, ECF Administrative Policies and Procedures, Section II.j, and the chambers' rules, with respect to filing documents under seal.

> The Court may modify the protective order in the interests of justice or for public policy reasons.

All stipulated protective orders shall be filed as a joint motion. The parties shall email directly to chambers a proposed order, in Word or WordPerfect format, containing the text of the protective order.

Procedure for Filing Documents Under Seal

No document may be filed under seal, i.e., closed to inspection by the public, except pursuant to a Court order that authorizes the sealing of the particular document, or portions of it. A sealing order may issue only upon a showing that the information is privileged or protectable under the law. The request must be narrowly tailored to seek sealing only of sealable material.

To file a document under seal, the parties must comply with this procedure:

A. The parties shall follow and abide by applicable law, including Civ. L.R. 79.2 and ECF Administrative Policies and Procedures, Section II.j, with respect to filing documents under seal.

B. The party seeking to file under seal must electronically file a "Motion to File Documents Under Seal" and electronically lodge the said documents using a new event called "Sealed Lodged Proposed Document." The System will inform the party that the documents will be sealed and only available to court staff. The Clerk's Office will indicate on the public docket that proposed sealed documents were lodged. A party need only submit a courtesy copy of the documents to chambers if the documents exceed 20 pages in length. If the court grants the motion to seal, the docket entry and documents will be sealed and designated on the docket as filed on the order date. If the court denies the motion to seal, the lodged documents will remain lodged under seal absent an order to the contrary.

C. The parties shall file a redacted version of the document sought to be filed under seal. The document shall be titled to show that it corresponds to an item filed under seal, e.g., "Redacted Copy of Sealed Declaration of John Smith in Support of Motion for Summary Judgment."

Courtesy

Be courteous and respectful at all times, in all settings. Counsel may expect such from the Court, and the Court expects such from counsel. Please be familiar with and abide by Civil Local Rule 83.4.

B. *Criminal Pretrial Procedures*

CRIMINAL PRETRIAL PROCEDURES

Please Note: The Court provides this information for general guidance to counsel. The Court may vary these procedures as appropriate in any case.

Inquiries on Criminal Matters

Judge Stormes' Courtroom Deputy ("CRD"), George Perrault, handles all inquiries on criminal matters. His telephone number is **(619) 557-7749.**

The Court's Schedule During Criminal Duty Week

During duty week the Court begins receiving new complaints and warrants in chambers at 9:00 a.m. More specific instructions for agents are posted on the Chambers door. Unless otherwise noted, morning calendar begins at 10:30 a.m. and afternoon calendar begins at 1:30 p.m. Dispositions are sometimes scheduled between 9:30 a.m. and 10:30 a.m.

Criminal Calendar (Non-Duty Weeks)

Criminal calendars on non-duty weeks are scheduled Tuesday and Thursday mornings from 9:30 a.m. until 12:00 noon, unless otherwise noted. Counsel are expected to be punctual and to advise the Court's CRD of any scheduling conflicts in advance of their hearing.

Motions To Modify Bond

Absent extraordinary circumstances, bail modification requests will not be heard unless calendared in advance and with 24 hours notice to the opposing party, Pretrial Services, and the sureties. Any documents to be proffered at the hearing must be provided to the Court's CRD 24 hours in advance of the hearing.

Stipulations (Joint Motions) for Change Of Bond Conditions

The Court will accept written stipulations for modification of bail conditions if they are in the form of a "joint motion"signed by all counsel, the defendant, the bond sureties, and the Pretrial Services Officer supervising the defendant. A copy of the Order of Conditions of Release must be attached to the joint motion and the filing party must submit a separate proposed order for the judge to sign. See CrimLR 1.1(e)(8); CivLR 7.2.

Presentation of Bond Documents

Counsel must present all bond documents in the form approved by the Court to Judge Stormes' CRD for review before bringing them to chambers. See Crim.LR. 46.1 for more information. The bond documents must include a copy of the Court's Order of Conditions of Release applicable to the defendant.

Material Witness bonds must include a notation, in the upper right hand corner of the bond, of the arraignment date and the initials of counsel for the material witness. Material witness bonds must also be presented to Judge Stormes' CRD for review.

Surety Examinations

Surety examinations will be heard only if calendared in advance with no less than 24 hours notice to the Court, all parties and the Pretrial Services Office. Defense counsel must provide the Court's CRD and the United States Attorney's Office with a copy of the proposed bail package, including in the case of a property bond, title documents, appraisals, bank loan statements and other relevant documents, 24 hours in advance of the hearing. With prior approval of the Court, out-of-state sureties may appear by telephone if they are accompanied by a notary to whom they can present a driver's license or other suitable identification.

Sentencing in Misdemeanor Cases

The Court generally requires a Presentence Report and Sentencing Summary Charts in Class A misdemeanor cases. See Crim.L.Rs. 32.1 and 58.2. In petty offense cases (e.g. misdemeanor illegal entry) where the defendant has a criminal history, the court requires a rap sheet prior to sentencing. Requests for immediate sentencing in misdemeanor cases are discretionary with the court.